Drawing Parallels

Quintin Lake

Drawing Parallels

Architecture Observed

Foreword by Richard Wentworth

PAPADAKIS

To those who build and the kindness of strangers

First published in Great Britain in 2009 by
Papadakis Publisher

PAPADAKIS

An imprint of New Architecture Group Limited

HEAD OFFICE: Kimber Studio, Winterbourne, Berkshire, RG20 8AN
DESIGN STUDIO & RETAIL: 11 Shepherd Market, Mayfair, London, W1J 7PG

Tel. +44 (0) 16 35 24 88 33
Fax. +44 (0) 16 35 24 85 95
info@papadakis.net
www.papadakis.net

Publishing director: Alexandra Papadakis
Editor: Sheila de Vallée
Editorial Assistant: Sarah Roberts

Front cover: Marble astronomical scale of the Samrat Yantra (the Supreme Instrument) is the world's largest sundial, standing 27 meters tall. Its shadow moves visibly at 1 mm per second at the Jantar Mantar, a collection of architectural astronomical instruments, built by Maharaja Jai Singh II between 1727 and 1734. Jaipur, India, 2002

Title page and frontis: *Shine through, shine out*; left: Detail of Lincoln Cathedral East window showing *The Creation and Redemption of Man*. Stained glass by Ward and Nixon, 1855. Lincoln, UK, 2004; right: Neon advertising lights above Nanjing East Road. Shanghai, China, 2007

ISBN 978 1 906506 04 9

A CIP catalogue of this book is available from the British Library.

Printed and bound in China

Contents

An Architecture of Looking

Some directions for use

Richard Wentworth

As you read this, look about you. Note the shapes and functions that surround you, the squares and right angles, the circles and cylinders, the coarse surfaces and the fine finishes. Try naming those materials – animal, vegetable, mineral.

The earliest ideas for *Drawing Parallels* were first generated by Quintin Lake over ten years ago when I happened to see a draft for a glossary of structures, buildings and architectural eventuality.

Even at that time, when a young student, Lake's desire to steer the compendium of his experience towards fresh audiences showed an exceptional clarity of purpose. I was struck by the way that all his images emerged from travel and encounter and articulated real experience in real time and space. Real conditions, real weather and real seasons. I remember thinking that perhaps the images could one day assemble themselves into a magnetic needle which would point a way across the whole puzzling field of cultural energy, the things which humans make and destroy, the things which humans leave behind, and the things which humans come upon. This is something that a good eye and a commitment to travel, not tourism, can set in motion.

The camera is a strange editorial tool – the world of 'seeing' has no edges, no right angles, only the marvels of peripheral vision and the edginess which is the gift of being human, that sensation of being curious and always wanting to know more than we can see. In English, this mongrel language, we are as likely to begin sentences with 'I think…' as with 'I feel…' and we often show our understanding of others by saying 'I see'. The camera can do none of this but editorial intelligence can. Our ability to do things comes as much from the gift of sight as from the capacity for thought. The eye, like the camera may be 'stupid', but it is the owner of the eye who makes 'pictures'.

Seeing, looking, watching, eyeing, observing, noticing, witnessing – together they add up to a prodigious critical process, one of the great things that all humans share. With the eye of Quintin Lake, you are reminded to look up.

He alerts you to both meanings, not just the spatial one, 'looking upwards', but also the pleasurable pursuit of information, or the tracking down of an acquaintance, whether a person, a building, or a space. He reminds you that the past is turning into the future. One verb, associated with vigilance, slips into a noun to remind us of the biggest question of all – time. In English, we may 'watch', but we also may wear one.

The object which you hold is another of those small, portable, architectural marvels – a book. A cousin of the hinge (and so a relation of both the door and the window) it pivots on its spine and allows a furling process, of befores and afters, of images and type, set in sequences that mirror, remind and rehearse. The reader (we don't say 'looker') brings to a book his own special powers of intervention and interpretation, moving back and forth through the territory before him. This too is how we become spatially intelligent, coursing to and fro in cities and beyond, acquiring our own thesaurus of spaces and places, as much as we map a sense of ourselves as temporary occupants of the world. We discover our 'whereabouts' surrounded by our 'belongings'. We learn to 'belong'.

All those questions of utility and serviceability, which architecture and urbanism can never escape, are played out in the utensils which populate our lives. Many of these mini architectures come with 'directions for use', whose counter-intuitivity thwarts and frustrates us.

Drawing Parallels is itself a utensil of a special kind, an un-guide book where the imagination which we associate with the promise of all books is the primary agent for giving directions. *Drawing Parallels* honours and dignifies the pleasure of inhabiting a haptic world. Its comparisons remind us how we come to differentiate between things, how we sort and re-sort. These multiple acts of recognition, which we store in our own reservoirs of experience, overflow into fresh conversations we come to share. It's unstoppable.

Hidden Harmonies:
The Photography of Quintin Lake

Hugh Cumming

This is an age of multiple images. We see more than has ever been seen. We hold more moments than have ever been recorded. Experience is almost lived when it is looked at. We think we understand when we look, and, having really, only glimpsed, we imagine we see all. Quintin Lake shows us what we have not seen. Then he celebrates it.

He is an alert eye at a time of tired acceptance, a swift penetrating iris of investigation that not only notices, but questions. He is the eye of the era of instant global access and the eye that travels on a jet plane. He has the enterprise and innocence of a 21st century tourist, with the sophistication of a consciousness steeped in the myriad vistas of centuries of diversity. He sifts through the kaleidoscope of shifting patterns, forms and statements, the chaos of ancient temples and brash contemporary insistencies, of delicate yet defiant monuments and unique urban feats, of slight unnoticed marvels and outrageous awe-inspiring conurbations, to find a passive beauty in the brutal, the spiritual in the functional, the outspokenly human and humane in the surreal landmarks of totalitarian and industrial decay. He has a coolly ironic perspective; he suddenly captures a connection, a pattern, a hidden harmony, a provocative witty mystery, a chilling mysterious enigma woven into what others would take for granted. And gradually we comprehend something that has never been seen, that has been there for aeons, or cast out, apparently randomly, in the brash crudity of a modern moment. We catch sight of something both very ancient and entirely of the moment, something cherished and something neglected, something we would not otherwise have, had he not found it and photographed it.

Even though each of his images stand as powerful composed comments in their own right, sometimes as engaging and intriguing glimpses of forms, details that, elsewhere, are magically, wholes, suddenly discovered and now acknowledged, follies or vernacular eccentricities, quaint oddities, once passed over, now claiming the foreground, close-packed aspects of ornament, suddenly flourishing as marvels, almost as intricate as the buildings they adorn, it is in the eloquent placing of two together that Lake's subtle linking of insight lies. "What interests me more is to pair two images to create an extra level of dialogue."

Lake is a photographer with an architectural training and sensibility; he has an acute sensitivity to form and space. But he does not simply, passively, represent architecture, as others intend it to be seen or understood. "...Most people's experience of 'famous' architecture is through photographs in books or magazines...so if you think of a seminal or classic building, it's often quite misleading as it doesn't show the context or the environment that it appears in..." He is aware that we receive our understanding and knowledge of so many buildings through an array of preordained images, incomplete, partial and constricted aspects of something deeper and more complex, and unrealised. He does not accept what is given, but is an iconoclast, seeking further levels of understanding, not just in a new image, but in the subtle statement that emerges. "I didn't quite trust the image portrayed, so searching for the image on the ground is what I'm trying to do."

His approach has its roots as much in the attitudes of the most natural of twentieth century photographers, Cartier Bresson. "The 'decisive moment' and going into a city on a kind of urban safari, the slightly macho pursuit of stalking round, waiting for a person to be perfectly framed between two buildings or a doorway in just the right light, that certainly interests me..." Certain projects will be the result of research and preparation, but it is what he finds through accident and discovery, through the open-mindedness and inspiration of a journey, that is really prized and telling.

Working on a separate commission in the Andes, Lake turned to notice a makeshift football pitch created by construction workers on the Interoceanic Highway. What caught his eye in particular was the pure form of the goal the men had built from bare tree trunks set in the expansive emptiness of the surrounding space, rather than the great natural one of the Andes. His image is an appreciation of one of those apparently arbitrary accidents that emerge from a combination of environment and enterprise. He catches a truth in the transitory, finds and fixes a statement in what might have otherwise have vanished. "The goal is just a temporary football pitch for road builders by a highway. They had just cleared a flat area next to their diggers and it's probably gone now... I stopped to look at a view in another direction and behind me... a pristine definition of space, high in the Andes with this very clean line. That appealed to me."

The image could stand alone, but what Lake chooses to employ is a simple yet profound device, which enables him to give all his insights and compositions far deeper resonance;"...as a photographer you can explore those multi layers of meaning and relish and enjoy that, and especially by comparing images. That gives even more scope to explore ambiguities..."These combinations of images, some with their own visual echoes or contrasting harmonies, form a commentary on the hidden histories and backgrounds of their subjects. Some work simply as surprising or unexpected similarities. The detail of a form will be apparent in something separated by a chasm of time and culture. Others incite you to examine what might otherwise be simply accepted in a single image:"... the beauty of photography and the pairing is that you can express things which words cannot express, and that's the tricky thing, as the intrigue of photography is expressing things you cannot say..."

In pairing the image of the goal post on the highway with an ancient Chinese doorway, both pictures take on a new dimension. These apparently disparate forms, an ancient and calculated crafting of space beside an arbitrary ephemeral structure suddenly draw together impulses and statements that cross divisions in the way only photography can."I enjoyed being a bit naughty by putting something built in ten minutes on the same level as something that was seen as the highest expression of a nation's art because there is a universality about what it was actually doing spatially."

Lake's vision of architecture as an organic composite of construction and cultural setting is partly derived from the inspirational revelations of Rudofsky's *Architecture without Architects:*"The freshness of the best pages, even after all this time, of images that you've never seen before, comparing totally different cultural interpretations..."This innovative approach to looking at architecture, and the way in which architecture is represented visually, is at the heart of Lake's outlook.

It is not just the images in themselves that are significant, but the way they are seen and received. This act of creating a commentary by contrasting or by simply comparing, by looking at the hidden and unacknowledged connections between forms was influenced partly by the approach of Richard Wentworth whose questioning iconoclastic assembly of form and image," started me wanting to express this photographically.""I like Wentworth's Thinking Aloud exhibition ... where he's compared a model of a German toy set in the 30s with a charcoal (drawing) of a shell burst by Keith Henderson in the First World War. Totally different contexts and media... but by taking the two we get closer to what an explosion is. So what this whole exhibition showed me is the power of the visual comparison in terms of provoking an idea."

Lake is sensitive to the particular harmonies of a place, the way the light, the ambience and the landscape create yet another form in conjunction with the buildings. In "Iran and Yadz specifically... the choreography of the domestic and religious buildings is masterful. It's like seeing a new colour for the first time for me." Yet he is equally appreciative of the strange brutal presence of a functional industrial building. These marginalised objects that are exiled to the outskirts of our awareness along with the hidden services they perform suddenly assume a new status where strange steel and concrete turrets reign over their peculiar industrial arenas. His real gift is in bringing both these landscapes together.

There is a strange harmonious serenity to a composition that contains an ancient Iranian wind tower overlooked by a delicate Tower of Silence. It is a mysterious scene in which these two forms are at one with the shape, colour and light of the landscape. The picture shows a composite relationship that is unique to an ancient culture. But Lake provocatively places this beside an image of a large sewage gate in Beckton, North London. It is bold, blatant and cumbersome. Yet, as Lake suggests, both are forms that are at once functional and unique, they have emerged from the necessary rituals that are integral to our lives, they are the shapes we give to what we may not wish to but must acknowledge. "The Iranian wind tower is the result of ...thousands of years of vernacular evolution and the result is exquisite, whereas the Beckton Tower is not like that, but there is a volumetric similarity... The building on the hill in the Iranian picture is a Zoroastrian Tower of Silence, so when people died they were taken up there and vultures would take their flesh away... they are both in the context of hugely important social systems which are to do with cleaning up the city; getting rid of dead bodies or getting rid of your waste."

These images bring us the hidden aspects of our world, they penetrate what has been covered with a lichen of time, indifference and familiarity, as much as what we have come to accept as the pattern of our present. His photographs of Pripiat, the abandoned town near Chernobyl which once held 40,000 people and which will remain irradiated for three hundred years, are so chilling and at the same time mysteriously optimistic they too could stand in their own right. The haunting presence of absence pervades its brutalist concrete avenues and vistas. "Emptiness and stillness and peace is something I'm very interested in getting across in my photographs, and architecture can lend itself to creating that atmosphere." A vacant and discarded chair speaks of everyone who has gone. "It's relentless tower block after tower block, after public building, for a whole town which has got nobody in it ... A city without people was much more physically moving than I'd expected." Yet on a balcony floor the slender trunk of a tree has emerged as if from a mysterious seed in the heart of the barren concrete: "... that tree is optimistic and inspirational and the seat is outward looking as well."

The picture is placed next to one of the ancient Ankhor temple where the roots of a giant tree seem to descend from the sky to crush the remnants of a building. "In Siem Reap the nature is dominant but in Pripiat nature is a fragile thing which is just trying to assert itself... they are both cities that have been destroyed in a certain way, and they are both cultures that are now gone, and they are separated by hundreds of years and totally different building materials..."

A picture of a gymnasium where benches and wall bars remain as paint falls in flakes is placed beside a shot of the strangely banal and almost innocuous facade of a school in Cambodia. Both are ordinary types common to cultures across the world, yet each holds a secret tragic past. "The S21 prison in Cambodia was a school before it was turned into a prison. Seventeen thousand people passed through there and only ten are known to have survived execution in this school... I think urban planners, designers, tend to think of a building's use under very fixed terms. .. but it's not at all fixed and photography is great to show fluidity of use."

The deceptive impression of surfaces leads continually to an awareness of illusion. Lake sees the sense of spectacle inherent in everything he observes. What is apparently permanent is presented as a kind of set. Observers in a gallery are matched with martialled tourists outside monuments. There are barriers between what is artifice and what is concrete, but these melt and shift. One moment they are there and in an instant they are indiscernible. In a former Soviet exhibition park, against the brute gestures of totalitarian monoliths, Lake finds two lovers, their indifferent and languorous pose almost an unconscious human act of rebellion. In the picture next to it, other lovers disappear in the long grass beside the banks of a river. In the haze of the idyll, almost as a distant shadow, a factory form seeps into their sightline on a distant bank. The image is a veil of illusions. The lovers are actors in a movie still, contriving their stance; the unseen valley, once the most contaminated in South America.

Public viewing binoculars overlooking the demilitarized zone on the border between North and South Korea form a visual boundary to the bizarre spectacle of observation. A hidden line delineates where you can stand in the so-called free world to peer into the masked realm of restraint beyond. This boundary between freedom and dictatorship is a no man's land of deceptions, the binoculars part of a permitted tourist package looking directly onto facsimile towns placed to deceive. Beside this we see the roadside barrier of the Interoceanic Highway, a zinc coloured metallic barrier with the painted bee-strip logo of a sign cutting across the vista of a mountain range. Here the march of urban development meets the majesty of nature. These are formal compositional barriers; they are cultural barriers too, almost merging into an emblem.

Then, finally, there are great urban images, the endless aerial sweeps of the cities of a future that is now, which almost dwarf any attempt to encompass their sheer scale and very nature in a visual image. How do you understand the dimension of something that has never been seen before and is at every moment breaking the very confines of your conception? These are awe-inspiring sights, celebrations of ultimate forms.

Quintin Lake not only traces patterns in traditional harmonies, he is tuned to the novel surprises of now, the bounty of a megalopolis, the radiant neon ornament of the brashest and the newest in the sapling turrets of an emerging superpower. He reaches over to the monuments of the biggest and the boldest to step suddenly across to something ancient and silent where man and nature have met and melded. He notices something obsolete in the most modern of concrete conurbations, something chillingly bereft that makes the freshest of architectural gestures old. And this is accomplished by these contemplative couplings, these deceptively simple contrasts with vistas that reach far beyond their beautifully composed surfaces. These are the parallels of the internet age, the emerging statements of the global moment, a wealth of visual relativism in which he has found undiscovered connections. These are carefully composed and crafted images which through this act of comparison hint at random truths. Some are straightforward celebrations of formal beauty, others are deeper revelations of darker political and ecological themes. Nothing is ever merely a message. Everything is always purely visual, yet open to ambiguity and enigma. This act of visual contrast is a reflection of the ironic clashes so particular to our time.

Seeing Shapes

I often think of that rare fulfilling joy when you are in the presence of some wonderful alignment of events. Where the light, the colour, the shapes, and the balance all interlock so perfectly that I feel truly over-whelmed by the wonder of it.

Charlie Waite

If architecture is the act of making shapes, from a detail to an overall impression, part of the art of photography is seeing and registering the wealth of changing forms and patterns that are created by the harmony and clash of buildings with their environments. The art of the contemporary photographer allows for the fine precision of focus on unnoticed, forgotten and ignored details which exist almost as structures in their own right. A doorway, a ceiling, a corner or a façade can come to life through the recognition of a composition. There are new forms, almost new works, created by the erosion of time. Decay and neglect fashion something fresh, whilst a fragment of a former whole achieves a revelatory beauty in its own right. This gallery of experience is new for each generation. The contemporary photographer not only notices and composes, but he can assemble to make unique modern statements.

Waves & Ripples

left: Lawn, railings and cobbles on Radcliffe Square viewed from St Mary's, the University Church. Underneath the square is storage space for the Bodleian Library, which contains around 600,000 volumes. Oxford, England, 2009

right: Detail of the concrete ribs which make up the façade of the Copan building, built by architect Oscar Niemeyer. São Paulo, Brazil, 2008

Corners expressed

left: Outer walls and moat of Nijō Castle. The raised corner used to house a five-storey tower which served as a look-out in 1750 but was not rebuilt. (Built from 1601 to 1626 by Tokugawa Ieyasu, founder of the Edo Shogunate). Kyoto, Japan, 2004

right: Corner of the three-tier marble terrace leading to the Hall of Preserving Harmony in the Forbidden City. (Built from 1406 to 1420). Beijing, China, 2007

Weathered composure

left: Granite rock formation near the summit of Glyder Fach. Wales, 2003

right: Göreme is a town of rock-cut dwellings that include troglodyte villages and underground towns – the remains of a traditional human habitat dating back to the 4th century. Cappadocia, Turkey, 1994

Buildings without precedent

left: Wind towers (Badgir) next to a building which acts as a refrigerator to store food and Zoroastrian Tower of Silence (Dakhmeh). Yazd, Iran 2007

right: Clean water flows into the Thames from the northern outfall of Beckton Sewage Treatment Works. Sewage from 3.4 million Londoners is treated on site every day. Barking Creek Tidal Barrier, which resembles a giant guillotine, was built over four years and completed in 1983. It is about 60m high, which allows shipping to reach the Town Quay in Barking further upstream. The barrier crosses the Barking Creek reach of the River Roding at its confluence with the Thames. London, UK, 2003

Site Line

left: Wood-lined gun embrasure of a German WWII bunker. The stepping form and wood lining were designed to minimise shrapnel entering the opening during an attack. Alderney, Channel Islands, 2006

right: Corridor in the Khas Mahal (white marble palace), a pavilion of imperial apartments in Agra Fort next to the River Yamuna. Agra, India, 2002

Lightly covered

left: Interior of the hexagonal conical dome of the Sheikh's tomb. Sheikh Abd as-Samad Mosque. Natanz, Iran, 2008

right: Great Dome of Saint Isaac's Cathedral, Built from 1818 to 1858. Under the Soviet government, the building was abandoned, then turned into a museum of atheism. Saint Petersburg, Russia, 2007

Glimpse of sky

left: Bricked up windows of a ruined façade in an abandoned building. Cordoba, Spain, 1993

right: Rock cut dwellings exposed by erosion and rock fall. Cappadocia, Turkey, 1994

Support systems

left: Supporting buttress preventing the collapse of the ruins at Llanthony Priory. Vale of Ewyas, Wales, 2009

right: Pine tree branch supported by a crutch which prevents collapse and controls growth to prevent twisting. The pine is seen as a symbol of good luck and longevity in Japanese culture. Imperial Park, Kyoto, Japan, 2004

Truncations

left: The remains of one of two Moorish style chimneys at Abbey Mills pumping station which gave the building a mosque-like appearance. They have not been used since steam power was replaced by electric motors in 1933. They were demolished during WWII because they were a landmark for German bombers on raids over the London docks. London, UK, 2003

right: Alau Minar minaret. Construction was stopped on the death of the Sultan, Alauddin Khilji in 1316, when it was 12m high. It was intended to be higher than its neighbour, Qutb Minar Minaret, the world's tallest brick minaret. Delhi, India, 2002

Numbered to fit

left: Stones on a reconstructed wall. Lille, France, 2002

right: Timber profiling blades in the Swindon Woodworking Workshop. Faringdon, UK, 2005

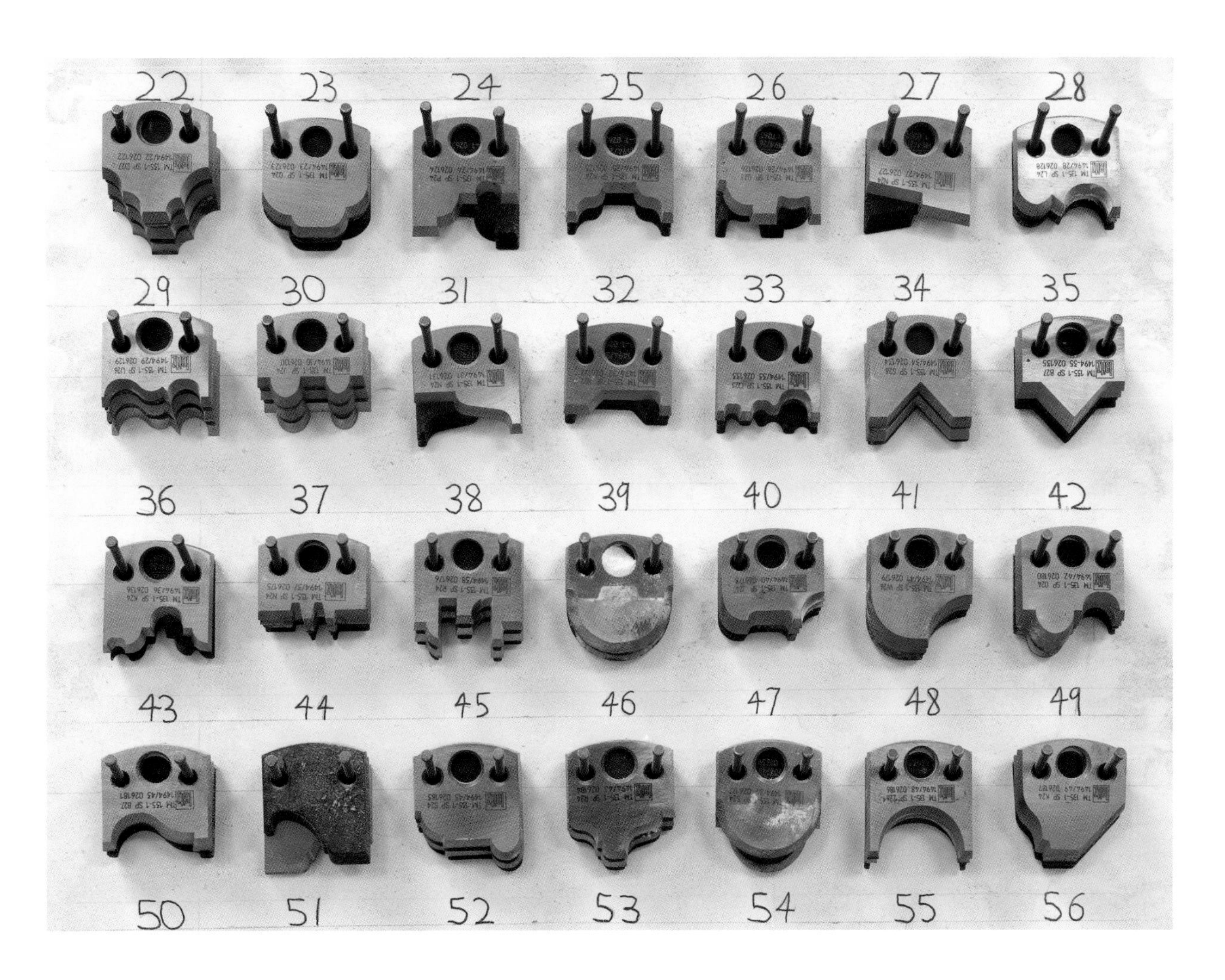
22
23
24
25
26
27
28
29
30
31
32
33
34
35
36
37
38
39
40
41
42
43
44
45
46
47
48
49
50
51
52
53
54
55
56

Historical standing

left: Old Blackfriars Railway Bridge piers and columns across the Thames. The bridge was used for the London, Chatham and Dover Railway in the 1860s but eventually proved too weak to support modern trains. London, UK, 2009

right: Archaic Doric column and capitals of the Temple of Hera, built around 550 BC by Greek colonists. It is the oldest surviving temple in Paestum, an ancient Greek, and later Roman city. The remains of the town are one of the best preserved examples of archaic Doric architecture. Paestum, Italy, 2001

Anticipated light

left: Honeycomb carved marble lattice screen in Agra fort. Agra, India, 2002

right: Rooflight in the dome of a bazaar. Yazd, Iran, 2008

Convergence

left: Underside of the stage of the theatre in the inner garden, Yuyuan Garden, originally built in the 14th year of the Guangxu reign in the Qing Dynasty, 1888. The old stage underwent extensive rebuilding in 2005. Shanghai, China, 2007

right: Ashley Building, School of Humanities, University of Birmingham. Architect: Howell, Killick, Partridge & Amis. Refurbished by Berman Guedes Stretton, Birmingham. UK, 2006

Framed void

left: Temporary football pitch for the road builders of the Interoceanic Highway next to a recently completed stretch of road. In the Andes near Cuzco, Peru, 2008

right: Vessel-shaped doorway in Yuyuan Garden, established in 1559. Shanghai, China, 2007

Channeling the flow

left: A pipe runs between two arches in an arcade in Bologna. There are some 38km of arcades in the city's historic centre, for which it is famous. Bologna, Italy, 2000

right: Ancient Roman drain constructed from interlocking ceramic pipe sections. Pompeii, Italy, 2001

Surface and Texture

Sometimes I enjoy just
photographing the surface because
I think it can be as revealing as
going to the heart of the matter.

Annie Leibovitz

Architecture has a texture. Whilst it is a commonplace that the very materials of buildings, both ancient and modern, contribute to their character, looking again at, or observing, the very fabric and substance of this aspect of the art, brings to life almost another art form in itself. For the photographer these architectural building blocks, from the smoothest marble to the roughest stone felt underfoot, from intricately glazed tiles to roughly cut timber in an ancient temple, merge into images where an alternative aesthetic is seen, beyond the functional or the decorative. The photographer can also register the elusive interplay of light with materials. It is in the bringing together of these moments, whether it is the natural vernacular of an ancient or traditional landscape with the neon radiance of a modern Chinese office block, that provides truly novel commentary.

Turned stone

left: Detail of terracotta column forming part of main entrance to the Romanesque Natural History Museum (1860 to 1880). The design was inspired by basalt columns at Fingal's Cave in western Scotland. Built by the architect Alfred Waterhouse. London, UK, 2008

right: Detail of sandstone lathe-turned balusters in Angkor Wat designed in the same style as the timber balusters of the surrounding buildings of ancient Khmer architecture. The 12th century temple was designed to represent Mount Meru, home of the devas in Hindu mythology. Angkor Wat, Cambodia, 2003

Underfoot

left: Roman brick floor laid in a basket weave pattern. Pompeii, Italy, 2001

right: The main road known as the Stradun, constructed entirely of marble in 1468 and reconstructed after the 1667 earthquake. The smooth surface reflects the street lights at night and becomes glass-like after rain. The city was shelled in 1991 to 1992 during the Croatian War of Independence. This left the street pock marked as can be seen at the lower left of the photograph. A more recent patina has been added by chewing gum and a pistachio shell. Dubrovnik, Croatia, 2005

Skyward Scribe

left: Calligraphy in florid thuluth script by Persian calligrapher Amanat Khan around the Pishtaq (main entrance) of the Taj Mahal. Jasper inlaid in white marble panels. The writing is slightly larger on the higher panels to reduce the skewing effect from below. The text is from YaSin, the 36th chapter of the Koran. Agra, India, 2002

right: Glazed tile Inscription dating from the 19th century in the northern iwan (semi-open space on the edge of a courtyard wall), Nasir-al-Mulk Mosque. Flexible timber, visible poking out of the wall at the top of the image, is used for earthquake resistance. The text is from Al Imran, the 3rd chapter of the Koran. Shiraz, Iran, 2008

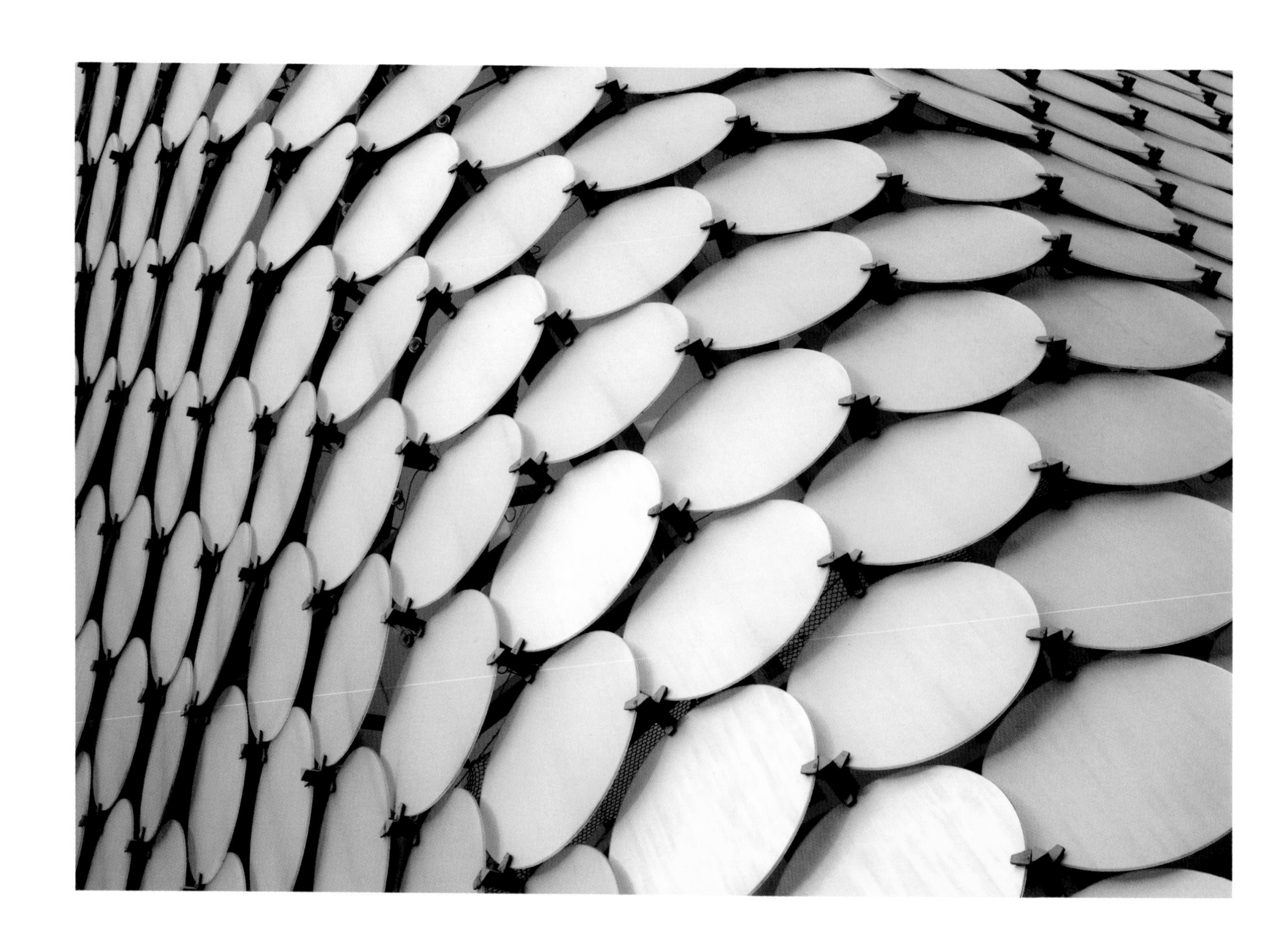

Pixilated skin

left: Glass disks on the façade of Galleria Fashion Store treated with iridescent foil on a metal support structure. A back-lit animated colour scheme ensures that the façade appears to be always changing by day and night. Architect: UN Studio. Engineer: Arup. Seoul, South Korea, 2007

right: Façade of Birmingham's Selfridges store at night. The skin consists of thousands of spun, anodised aluminium discs that reflect the surrounding city, set against a blue curved, sprayed concrete wall. Architect: Future Systems. Engineer: Arup. Birmingham, UK, 2007

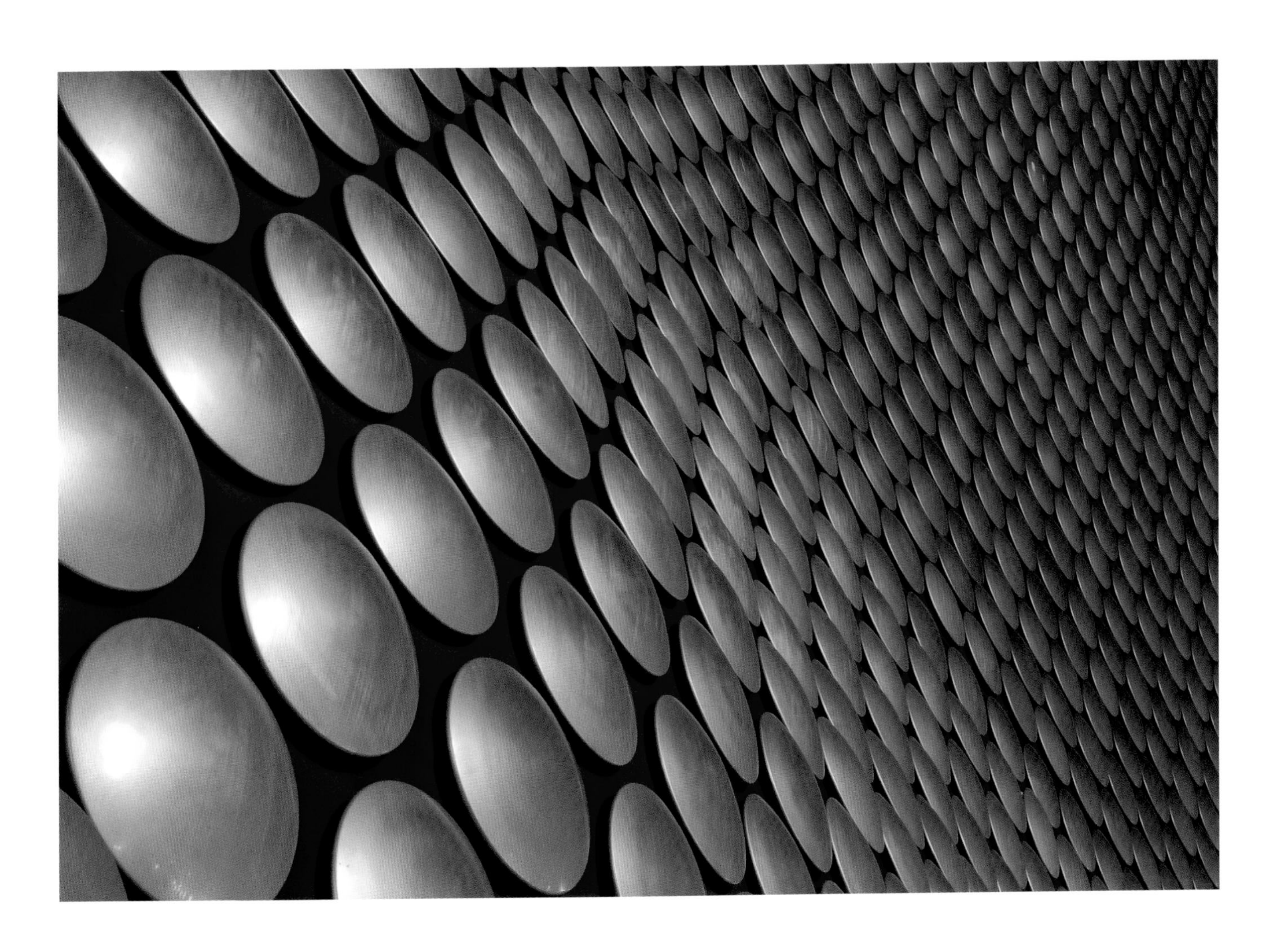

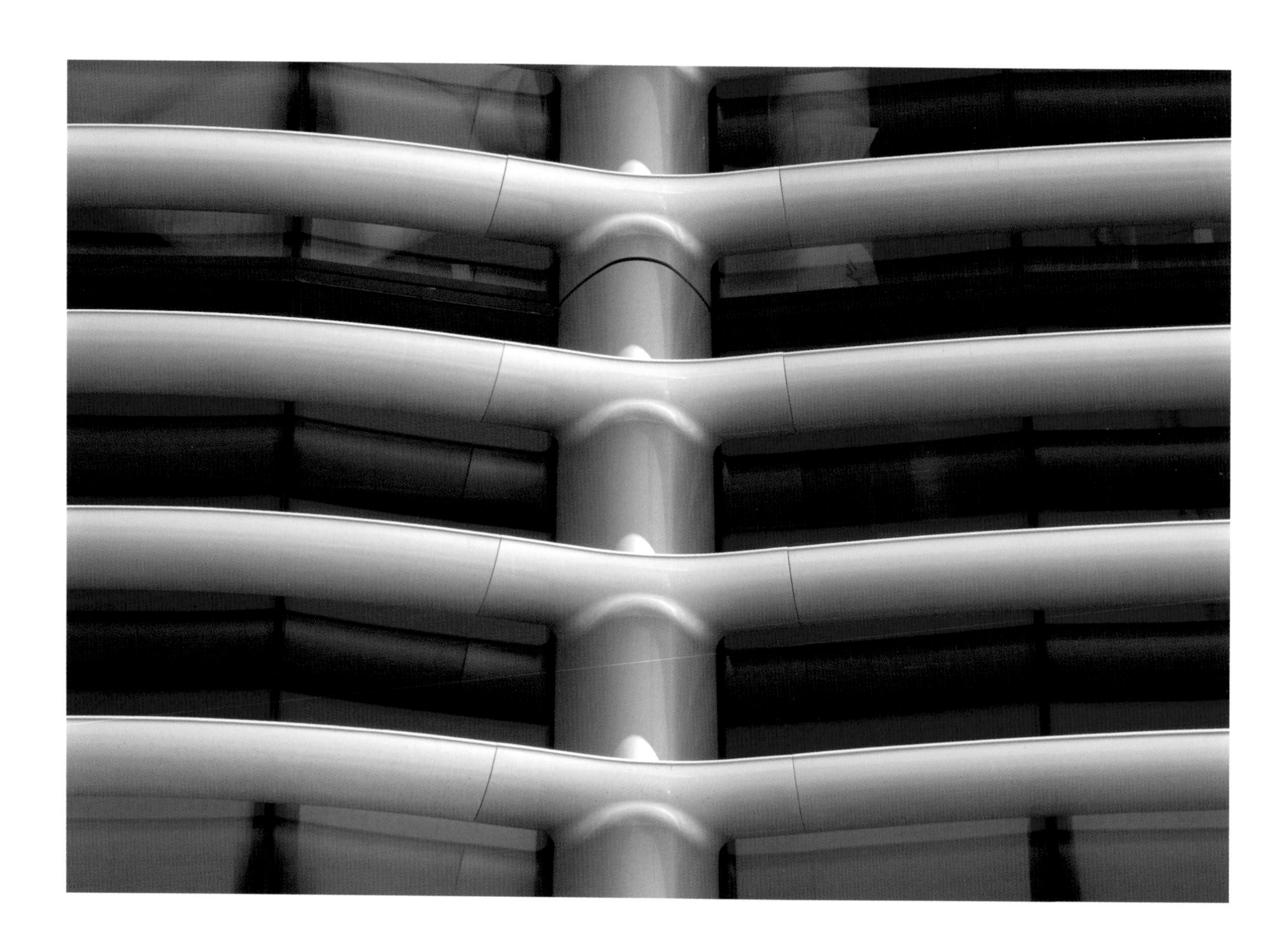

Aligned

left: Solar shades on The Walbrook constructed of fibre-reinforced polymer with an automotive finish – making the sheen resemble that of a car. Architect: Foster + Partners. Engineer: Arup. London, UK, 2009

right: Bamboo fence opposite Nijō Castle built in the Kennin-ji style after the temple of the same name. Kyoto, Japan, 2004

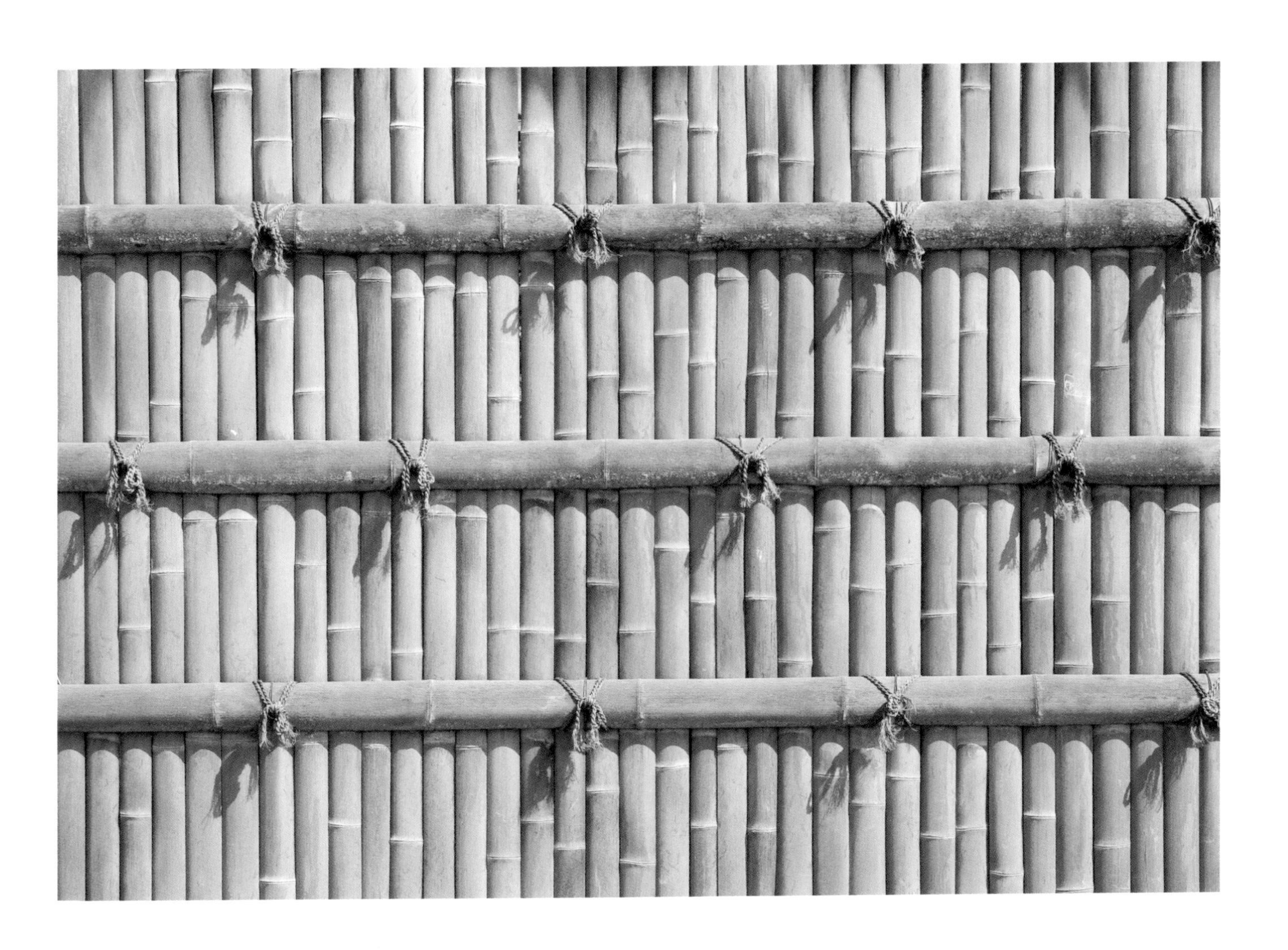

Audible access

left: Detail of door to the East Gate of the Temple of Heaven (1406-20). The Ancient Chinese regarded odd numbers as masculine and even as feminine. Nine represented the "ultimate masculine" and was symbolic of the supreme sovereignty of the Emperor. The gates have studs arranged in a nine by nine grid. Beijing, China, 2007

right: Townhouse door knockers. The masculine door knocker on the left is heavy and makes a loud sound, indicating a man's arrival. The feminine door knocker is ring-like and makes a lighter sound, announcing a woman. Islamic custom dictates that men and women should not interact unless they are married or related. Yazd, Iran, 2008

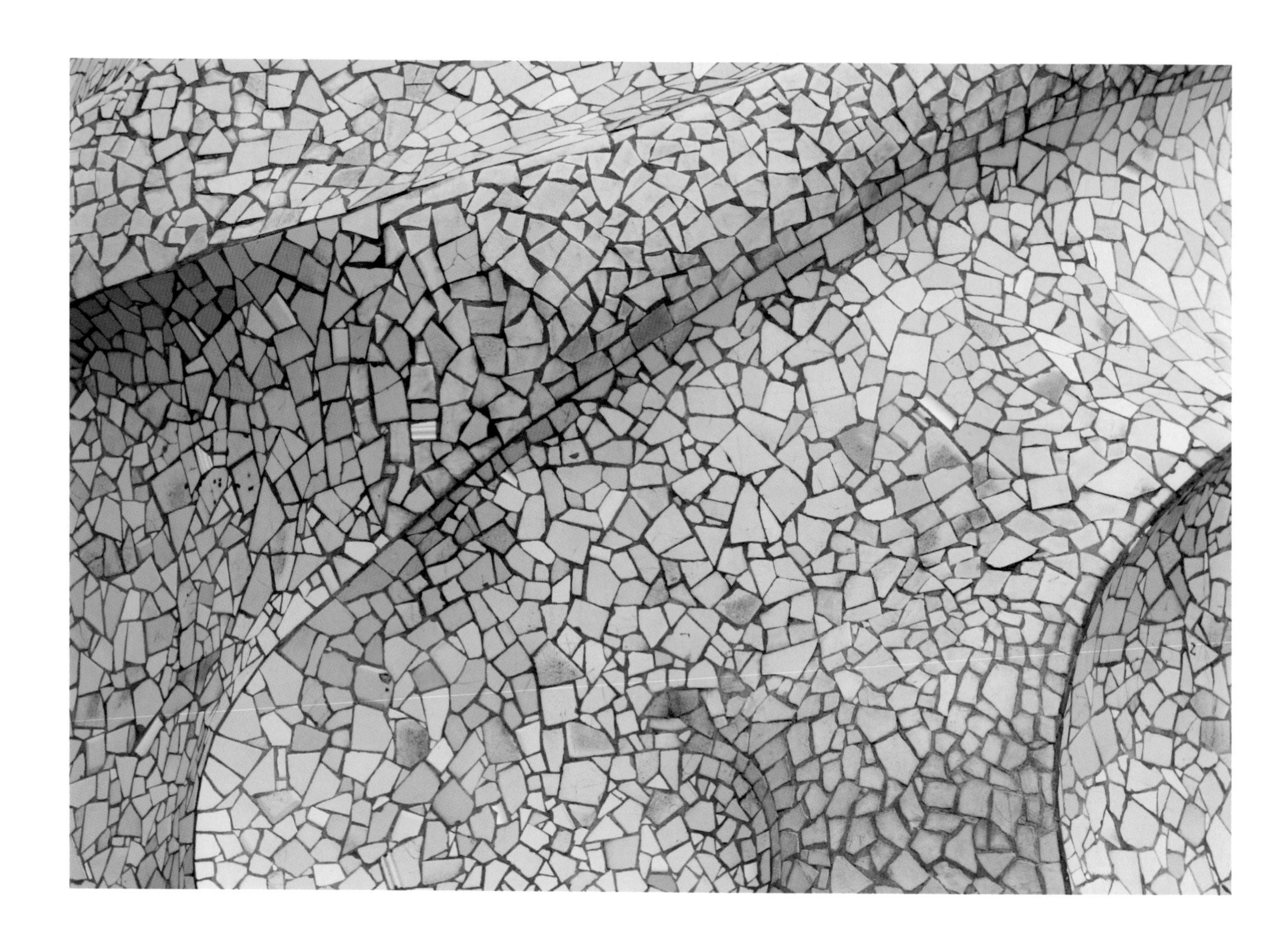

Bits and pieces

left: Detail of sculptured spiral stair exits faced with broken ceramics and marble on the roof terrace of Casa Milà, better known as La Pedrera (Catalan for 'The Quarry'). Built 1906-1910. Architect: Antoni Gaudí. Barcelona, Spain, 2003

right: Detail of a wall of recycled electrical fittings in Nek Chand's Rock Garden. From 1957 he secretly collected stones, metal, bricks, and other waste from Le Corbusier's building sites. When discovered in 1975, it had become a 12-acre (49,000sq.m) complex of interlinked courtyards, filled with hundreds of pottery-covered, concrete sculptures of dancers, musicians, and animals. Chandigarh, India, 2002

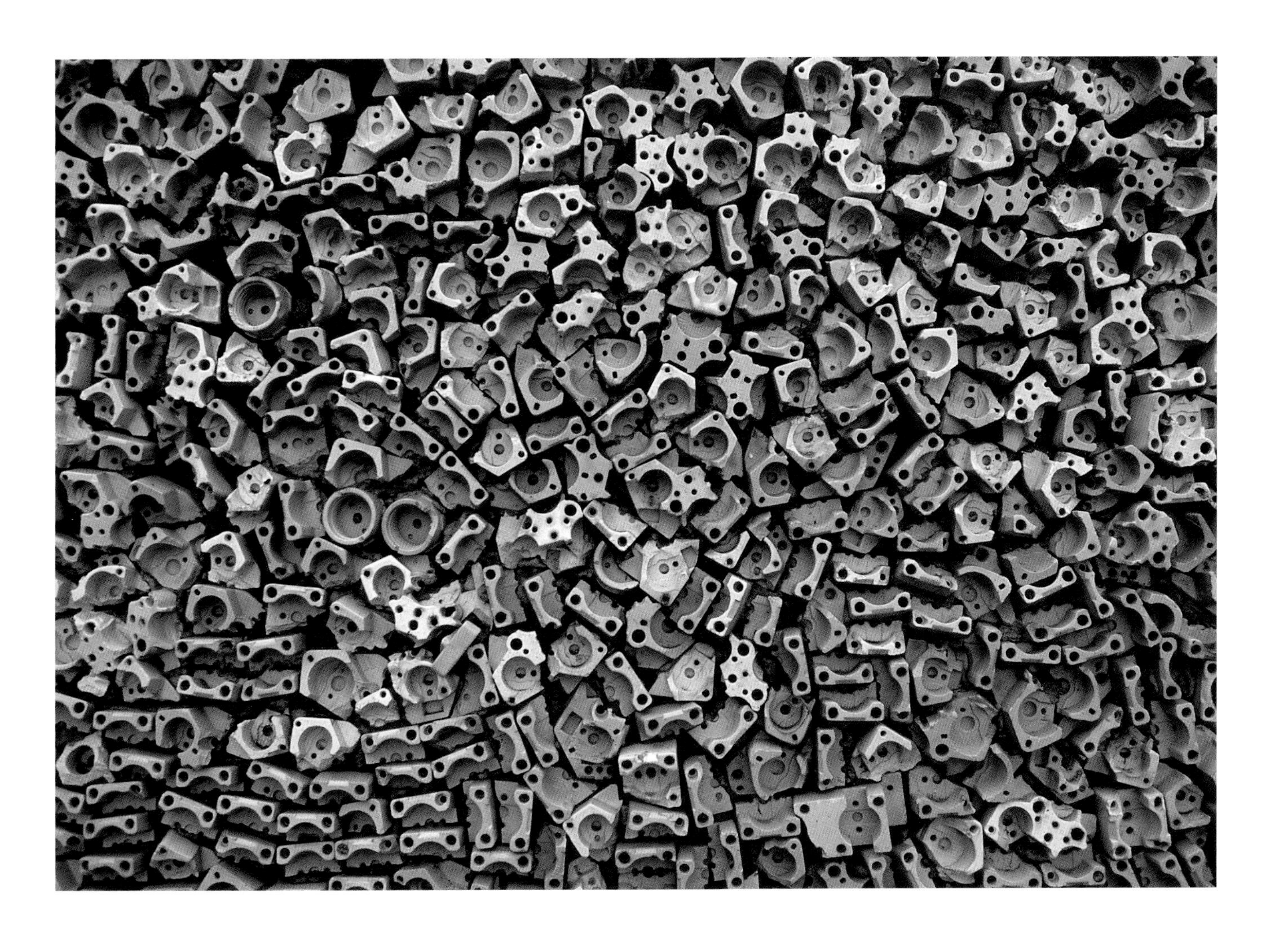

Overlapped

left: Timber roof tiles of the Refectory (Trapezna) of St. John the Divine in St. Michael's Golden-Domed Monastery. Kiev, Ukraine, 2007

right: Red tiles, shaped and patterned like fish scales, on the roof of the National Museum of Cambodia, constructed 1917-24 and inspired by Khmer temple architecture. The roof tiles have sections offset for ventilation, which incidentally provide entry and exit points for bats. For years the building was infested with bats and until 2003 it housed the world's largest bat enclave – numbering two million – inside a man-made structure. Phnom Penh, Cambodia, 2003

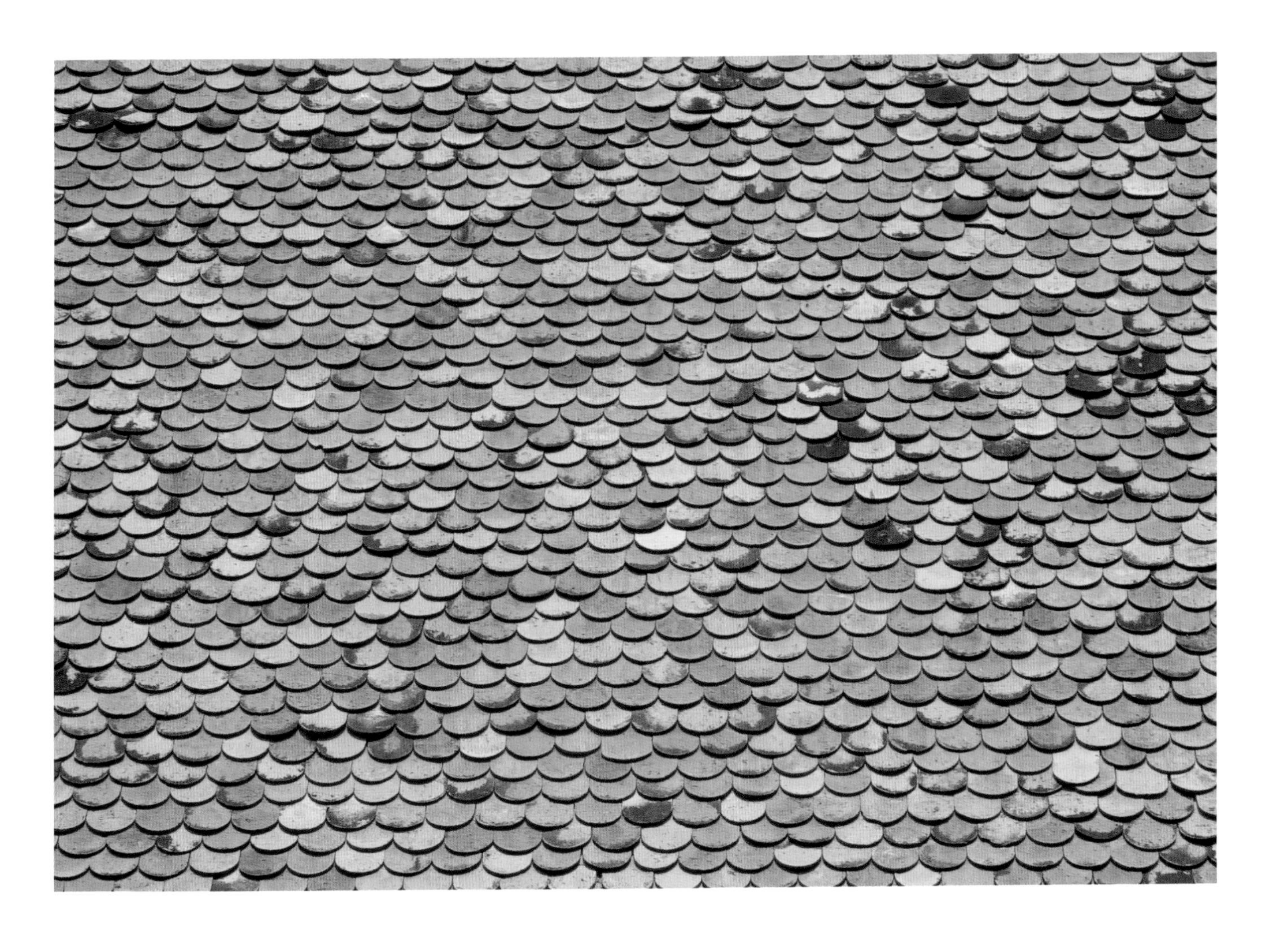

Interrupted edge

left: Detail of the edge of a Roman wall. The flat red bricks make up the edge and the wall is in-filled with the diamond-shaped, grey bricks. Pompeii, Italy, 2001

right: Koto-In Buddhist temple, detail of tatami mat and shōji (paper) screen runners. The edge of the tatami mat is finished with linen bearing a 'Kourai Beri' design (Korean pattern). In polite society the edging was not walked on when moving around the room. Kyoto, Japan, 2004

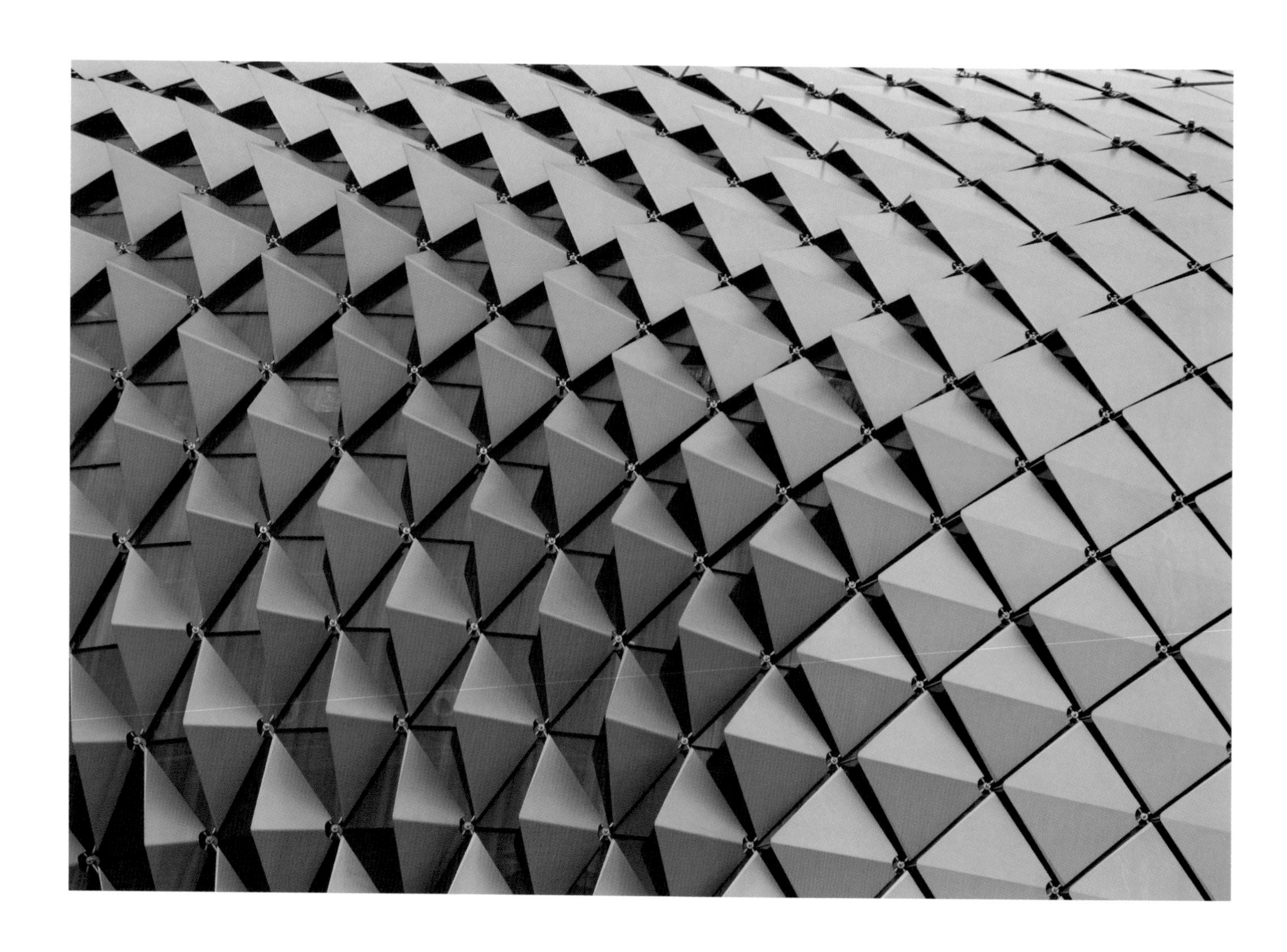

Responsive skin

left: Detail of aluminium sunscreens on the façade of the Esplanade, Theatres on the Bay, Singapore. The shields are set to be more open or closed depending on the angle at which the sun hits them, affording the glass façades protection from direct sunlight without limiting the view. Many Singaporeans casually refer to the Esplanade as the Durian because of its resemblance to the tropical fruit. Architect: Michael Wilford & Partners & DP Architects Singapore. Singapore, 2003

right: Timber roof tiles of an alpine hay barn, South Tyrol, Italy, 2002

Reflected identity

left: The Arsenal reflected in the façade of the State Kremlin Palace. Architect: Michael M. Poshokin. Moscow, Russia, 2007

right: Façade of 30 St Mary Axe, also known as the Gherkin, at dusk. The double façade creates a natural ventilation system and giant double glazing effect; air is sandwiched between two layers of glazing and insulates the office space inside. The triangulated perimeter structure is structural and adds to the buildings rigidity. Architect Foster + Partners (2004). Engineer: Arup. London, UK, 2009

Fractured geometries

left: Knapped flint wall. Norwich. UK, 2001

right: Detail of geometrical timber design on the door of Masjid-e-Jamé Mosque. Yazd, Iran, 2008

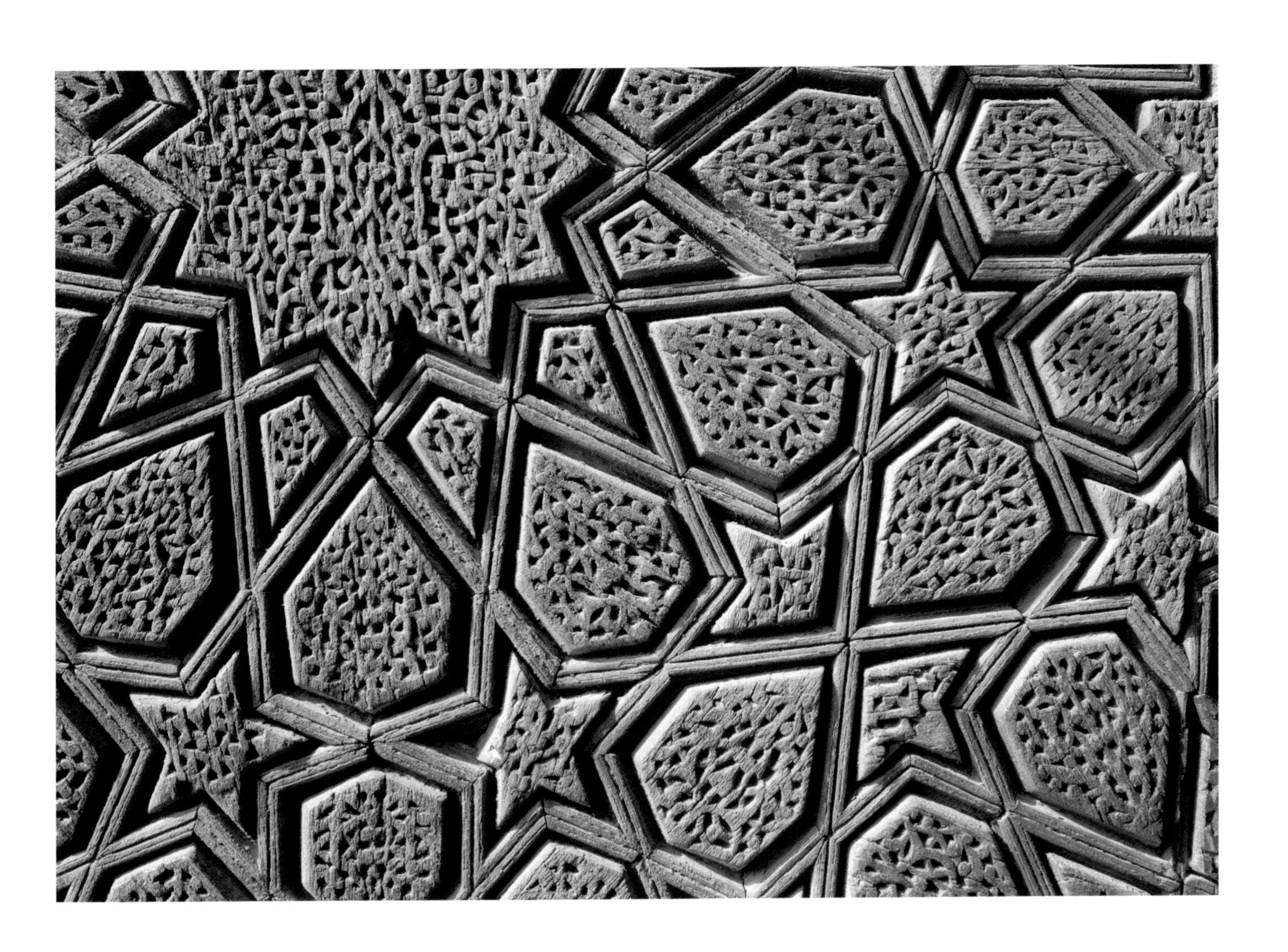

Wall of words

left: Neon signs advertising Huntley Clock and Watch and an optician. Shanghai, China, 2007

right: Detail of glazed tile and terracotta script view of khanqah portal on the right flank of the 13th century Shaykh 'Abd al-Samad Shrine complex. The central part is made up of a square kufic pattern meaning "There is no God but Allah, Mohammed is the prophet of God and Ali is the Imam from Allah." The left script reads "in the year of sixteen." The sentence is incomplete. Natanz, Iran, 2008

Rooftop scales

left: Lead covered domes on the Mihrimah Camii Mosque complex, Istanbul, Turkey, 1993

right: One of the few original roof tiles in Dubrovnik, Croatia. The city known as the Pearl of the Adriatic was heavily shelled during the break-up of Yugoslavia in 1991. During the siege of Dubrovnik two-thirds of the town's old buildings were damaged. Today the roofs are a patchwork of restored and original tiles. The traditional clay tiles were originally shaped over a man's thigh. Dubrovnik, Croatia, 2005

Perforations

left: A boy in the opening of a finely carved window in the Arg (citadel) of Karim Khan, Shiraz, the home of Persian romantics and poets. Shiraz, Iran, 2008

right: Arrow slits in the Tower of London's outer curtain wall built by Edward I between 1275 and 1285. London, UK, 2009

Organising Space

Architecture is the will of an
epoch translated into space.

Mies van der Rohe

The organisation of space is the realm of both architect and photographer. The nature of space, and the very means by which we recognise it, is always fluid and transitory. The photographer not only recognises great established relationships between familiar structures and their environment, but also observes the constantly evolving realignments or mutations, which exist between tradition and modernity, as much as between manmade structures and nature. There are moments of random interaction between humanity and the great landscapes of the natural world where an almost instinctive relationship can be captured in something as simple as a workmen's goal mouth by a highway. Barriers, enclosures, walls and routes are not just overt structures but unspoken strictures. These attempts at definition and containment speak of deeper cultural and political truths. By looking at them, by bringing them together, hidden realities and sinister webs of power are gradually revealed.

Absolute boundaries

left: Tourist viewing platform for looking into North Korea from the South Korean side of the 38th parallel. Situated on top of Dorasan (Mount Dora), the observatory looks across the Demilitarized Zone. It is the part of South Korea closest to the North. Mount Dora, South Korea, 2007

right: Road barrier above a steep drop at the edge of a newly completed section of the Interoceanic Highway in the Peruvian Andes. Above Cuzco, Peru, 2008

Related scale

left: Children's benches, Sculpture Park, also known by the expatriate name Fallen Monument Park, Moscow, Russia, 2007

right: The Hungarian Parliament Building built in a gothic revival style from 1896-1904 seen through the arches of the Halászbástya or Fisherman's Bastion, Buda Castle. Budapest, Hungary, 2005

Altered face

left: Montezuma Castle National Monument Cliff dwellings built and used by the Pre-Columbian Sinagua people around 1400 AD. The five-storey stone and mortar dwellings contain 20 rooms and once housed about 50 people. A natural overhang shades the rooms and shelters them from rain. Camp Verde, Arizona, USA, 1990

right: The tombs of the Achaemenid kings Darius 1, Artaxerxes 1 and Xerxes 1 (l. to r.) carved out of the rock face from 4-500 BC. The entrance to each tomb at the centre of the cross opens onto to a small chamber containing the king's sarcophagus. The façades are thought to be replicas of the entrance of the palace at Persepolis. Fars, Iran, 2008

Vertical values

left: Office tower and apartments. Hong Kong, China, 2004

right: Edifício São Vito, on the eastern edge of São Paulo's downtown. The building was abandoned and then invaded by squatters. It is sometimes referred to as a vertical favela. São Paulo, Brazil, 2008

Step and repeat

left: Q'allaqasa, the citadel of Inca Písac lies atop a hill at the entrance to the valley. The Inca's agricultural terraces are still in use today. They enabled them to produce more food than would normally be possible at 11,000ft. The narrow rows of terraces are thought to represent the wing of a partridge (pisaca). Pisac, Peru, 2008

right: An ice house or Yakhchal, an ancient refrigerator allowing the storage of ice in the desert in summer. It was collected in winter and kept cool by its shape and walls made from special mortar called s_rooj, composed of sand, clay, egg whites, lime, goat hair, and ash, which was resistant to heat transfer. Abarqu, Iran, 2008

ایزوگام پیروز دلیجان
۰۹۱۳۶۵۱۱۲۱۸
۰۳۵۱-۳۵۶۳۵۶۰۱۹

Looking inwards

left: A disused caravanserai on the road from Yazd to Isfahan. The buildings served as a roadside inn for travellers. They provided security and each merchant stayed in one of the identical bays with the square used for animals. Iran, 2008

right: The Amphitheatre of Pompeii is the oldest surviving Roman amphitheatre. It hosted gladiatorial games and other events. Seating was divided into three distinct social groupings and protection from the sun was provided by velaria suspended above the crowd from the top of the arena. The amphitheatre was buried by the eruption of Vesuvius (visible behind) in 79 AD. Pompeii, Italy, 2001

Defining shadows

left: A large rock shelter its surface scattered with Middle Stone Age artefacts. The walls containing a number of Bushman Rock paintings recorded during the Lesotho Rock Art Survey, 2000. Lesobeng Valley, Lesotho, 2000

right: Shadow of the belltower of Saint Sophia Cathedral across Bohdan Khmelnytsky Square. Kiev, Ukraine, 2007

Linear access

left: Internal corridor between the split-level apartments of the Unité d'habitation built in 1963 by Le Corbusier. Briey-en-forêt, France, 2005

right: Victory Park Metro Station opened in 2003. Moscow, Russia, 2007

Corralled

left: Workers' camp on the Interoceanic Highway. Peruvian Andes, 2008

right: A corral of llamas on the high Puna at approx. 4000m in the Andes. Peruvian Andes, 2008

Enveloping form

left: Scaffolding surrounding the second temple of Hera. The Greek Doric temple was built in about 450 BC. Paestum, Italy, 2001

right: Statue of Lenin at Sculpture Park (Fallen Monument Park), Moscow, Russia, 2007

Road edge

left: The Interoceanic Highway runs across freshly deforested rock cut into gigantic terraces to try to control rock fall. Sometimes these terraces extend many hundreds of metres up the mountain. Andes, Peru, 2007

right: Cars parked along a pavement. Prague, Czech Republic, 2006

Ceremonial hierarchy

left: Stepped Throne of the Incas cut into the Rodadero, a giant diorite rock hill, exactly opposite Sacsayhuamán, an Inca walled complex built in the 15th century near the old city of Cuzco, at an altitude of 3,701m. Its function prior to the conquest remains a mystery. But if the outcrop represents the back of a snake, as has been suggested, the throne is riding on its back. The throne faces east towards the rising sun, which was of the greatest importance to the Inca. Cuzco, Peru, 2008

right: Photographs of catholic hierarchy from the Pope to the altar of Igreja Nossa Senhora Aparecida. Cubatao, Brazil, 2008

BENTO XVI

Fissure

left: Path through the rubble of demolished houses that are still inhabited before the construction of new buildings. Shanghai, China, 2007

right: Path through an overgrown lawn. Stockwell, London, UK, 2009

28

Protected access

left: The remains of Milecastle 39, also known as Castle Nick, on the Whin Sill. The former barracks was part of the defences of Hadrian's Wall, built by the Romans across the width of England from AD 122-8. Northumberland, UK, 1998

right: Defensive wall and its surroundings built from the 8th to the 16th century. Dubrovnik, Croatia, 2005

Concrete expression

left: Glen Canyon Dam on the Colorado River. Damming the river flooded Glen Canyon and created a large reservoir called Lake Powell. Built 1956-66.
Page, Arizona, USA, 1990

right: Raised concrete road at dawn. Shanghai, China, 2007

Shelter and Home

All architecture is shelter,
all great architecture is the design
of space that contains, cuddles,
exalts, or stimulates the persons
in that space.

Philip Johnson

Photography captures both the visual appearance and the hidden intent inherent in a building. However transitory or ephemeral the structure, we can see the impetus for human survival in the act of creating a shelter, whatever the material, whether it is as ancient and fundamental as stone and wood, or as modern and widespread as glass, concrete and plastic. The fact that a dwelling embodies a more complex range of impulses, a strange mixture of domesticity and adornment, a basic expression of identity, in what can only be hinted at in the concept of home, forms the secret emotional dimension to architecture that emerges in the photograph. This is another landscape, beyond function and form, an emotional and psychological aspect that is only just beginning to be charted in these far-reaching visual connections.

A door & two windows

left: The home of D. Maninha, aged 94, one of the oldest inhabitants.
Pylons, Cubatão, Brazil, 2008

right: Thabang and family outside their home in Ha Motenalapi in the Senqunyane valley. They are wearing their Basotho tribal blankets. The door and window mouldings demonstrate Litema, the mural art of the Basotho. The hut floor and window mouldings are made from Daga, a mix of earth and dung. The high ammonia content of the dung acts as an antiseptic. The patterns engraved around the doorways may represent the surrounding furrowed fields. Ha Motenalapi, Lesotho, 2000

Rotundas

left: The cathedral of Saint Peter in Vysokopetrovsky Monastery was one of the first rotundas in Russian architecture. Built in 1517. Moscow, Russia, 2007

right: A tufa fairy tower dwelling in Cappadocia sculpted by wind and flood water. Turkey, 1993

Two of a kind

left: Big Chute Marine Railway, a ship lift at Lock 44 of the Trent-Severn Waterway in Ontario. It works on an inclined plane to carry boats in a cradle over a change 18m high. Although a conventional lock would have been simpler, the marine railway was chosen to prevent the possible migration of sea lamprey from Georgian Bay into the Trent-Severn system. Built in 1977. Ontario, Canada 1990

right: Two caravans on Akerman Road, Camberwell. London, UK, 2009

Room with a view

left: Jag Mandir palace viewed across Pichola Lake framed by a window in Shiv Niwas Palace, Udaipur. Rajasthan, India, 2002

right: A boulder framed by a tent opening, at the foot of Hvannadalshnúkur mountain on Vatnajökull glacier. Skaftafell National Park, Iceland, 1999

Sheltered & exposed

left: A house surrounded by banana plants in Jardim São Marcos favela. Cubatão, Brazil, 2008

right: The Gallarus Oratory (Irish: Séipéilín Ghallarais meaning "The Church of the Place of the Foreigners") is believed to be an early Christian church built between the 6th and 9th centuries. It has a corbelled roof and is built with stones laid at a slight angle – lower on the outside than on the inside – to allow rainwater to run off and thus keep the interior relatively dry despite the lack of mortaring. The building has remained in excellent condition for 1300 years. Dingle Peninsula, Ireland, 1991

Smooth with the rough

left: One of 500 or so 19th century wooden buildings in Riga. Latvia, 2007

right: Alpine hay barn. South Tyrol, Italy, 2002

Introvert or extrovert

left: A Japanese lacquer shop. Kyoto, Japan, 2004

right: General Store Acrijur. Cubatão, Brazil, 2008

BAZAR - PAPELARIA - CONFECÇÃO
Acrijur
CAMISETAS-UNIFORMES ESCOLARES - ARTIGOS P/ PRESENTES
BAZAR - PAPELARIA - CONFECÇÃO
Acrijur
CAMISETAS-UNIFORMES ESCOLARES - ARTIGOS P/ PRESENTES
TEL: 3361-2698
3361-7125
BAZAR PAPELARIA
CONFECÇÃO
A TODOS OS
AMIGOS E CLIENTES
Feliz Natal e
Ano Novo
AQUI TEM
ADT
Compre aqui com
VISA
VISA Electron

Toe in the water

left: Buyong-jeon pleasure pavilion in the Biwon or secret garden in Changdeok-gung palace. It is cantilevered over the edge of a lotus pond with two pillars in the water. The garden was first landscaped in 1623 and served for centuries as a royal retreat. Seoul, South Korea, 2007

right: Vila dos pescadores favela on the banks of the Casquerio River. Cubatão, Brazil, 2008

Splendid isolation

left: Gonbad Ali Dome tomb tower. Abarqu, Iran, 2008

right: Chastleton House dovecote built of Cotswold stone in the 17th century. Chastleton, UK, 2007

Tree house

left: Tree house in the South Tyrol Alps. Italy, 2003

right: Town house with Japanese black pine tree which also may act as a barrier to prevent people climbing over the outer wall. The curved structure is an inuyarai (a lightweight removable bamboo screen) to prevent rain splashes from the ground hitting the wall and causing the timber to rot. Kyoto, Japan, 2004

Telegraphing intent

left: Branch of the Industrial and Commercial Bank of China with apartments above. Shanghai, China, 2007

right: Wakuden Restaurant. Reinforced concrete and chestnut timber. Architect: Kishi Waro, K Associates. Kyoto, Japan, 2004

歩行者
自転車専用

Tropical shelter

left: Silvinha's house, Jardim São Marcos favela. Cubatão, Brazil, 2008

right: A shop adjacent to the Interoceanic Highway. Quince Mil, Peru, 2008

Memory and Place

Memory is not an instrument for exploring the past but its theatre. It is the medium of past experience, as the ground is the medium in which dead cities lie interred.

Walter Benjamin

A place is not a conglomeration of functional structures. Where we live, visit or observe, and the images we form and receive of it, gains its real nature from the feelings identified with it. An empty brutalist cityscape and an abandoned school gym, can speak of a more tragic dimension to our lives that is somehow inscribed in the very essence of a place. The way that vanished cultures persist in traces of their legacy, that nature reclaims vast human endeavours, that modern cruelty and power leave an aura or a sense of their very character in an ambience, is something that the photographer can capture. There are deeper, almost intangible remnants, some hauntingly sad, some joyful, that emerge as visual shocks or surprises, to be seen in the frozen image of a photograph. The chilling catastrophe of an abandoned city bereft of humanity clashes, paradoxically, with the defiant optimism of resurgent nature.

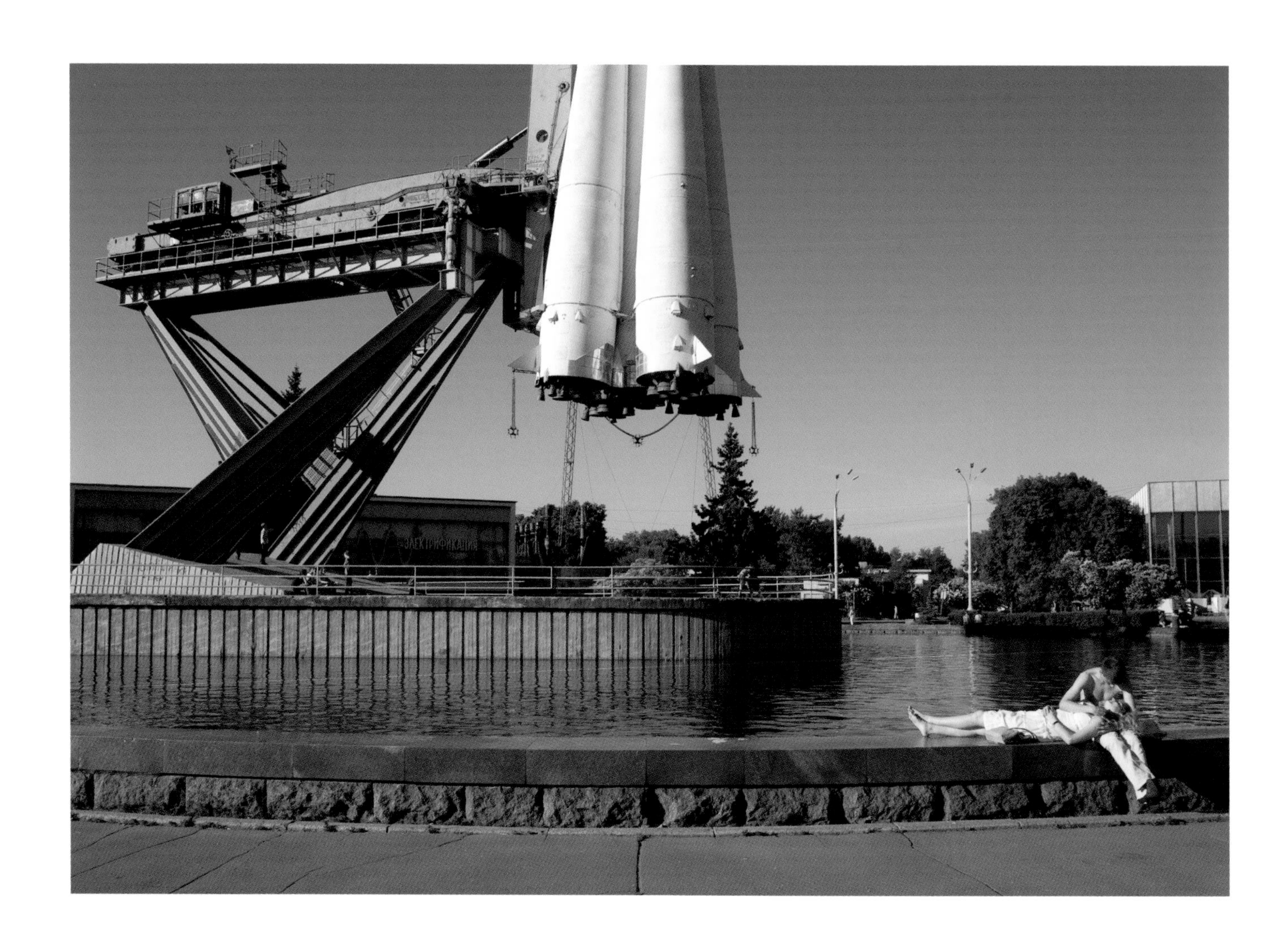

Emotional geography

left: A couple below an R-7 Rocket, an exact copy of the launcher that blasted off in 1961 with the first man in space, Yuri Gagarin. Part of the All-Russian Exhibitions Centre, previously named Exhibition of Achievements of the National Economy (VDNKh). The rocket was part of the Space Pavilion, one of 82 pavilions on the site. Moscow, Russia, 2007

right: Tailani Souza & Chris Dukes at dusk by the Fosfertil factory during the filming of *Holidays in Cubatão*, directed by Rubens Azevedo. Cubatão, Brazil, 2008

Memorial stone

left: Grave stone, Tende cemetery. Tende, France, 1992

right: Graves of princes and members of the royal household in the Saadian tombs. Marrakech, Morocco, 1998

Faceless

left: *House*, sculpture by Rachel Whiteread. London, England, 1993

right: A dry fuel storage facility built in 1999 but later found to be unsuitable for some of the Chernobyl fuel assemblies because they had cracked, soaked up water, changed shape. The facility now stands idle. Pripyat, Ukraine, 2007

Addressing identity

left: Disused doorbell in housing. Venice, Italy, 1991

right: Doorbells for apartments. Budapest, Hungary, 2005

MEGYERI
SOMOGYI JÓZSEF
Dr. Tóth Pál
BUZÁSI
MEGYERI
Buzási
BUJTOR
L ESZAY DANIEL
STRASSZ
MULADI

Lost in the jungle

left: Sandstone and laterite blind window in Beng Mealea Temple, built in the early 12th century. Siem Reap, Cambodia, 2003

right: A derelict Portuguese hospital in the jungle above Cubatão. Brazil, 2008

Reclamation

left: A doorway in Ta Prohm to a temple built in the late 12th and early 13th centuries as a monastery and university. The door is surrounded by silk cotton tree roots encased by strangler figs roots, which develop their own underground root system. They then grow quickly, often strangling the host tree, which in time dies and rots away. The strangler fig continues to exist as a hollow tubular lattice that provides shelter for many forest animals. Siem Reap, Cambodia, 2003

right: A silver birch tree growing through the floor on the terrace of the Hotel Polissia 21 years after the Chernobyl disaster. Pripiat, Ukraine, 2007

Absence

left: An area of low-rise housing is demolished for development. The writing on the wall reads, "Overusage of Electricity Prohibited". Shanghai, China, 2007

right: World Trade Center, built 1966-73, destroyed in 2001 killing 2,750 people. The tube-frame design allowed open floor plans as the loads were carried via perimeter columns forming a Vierendeel truss. Architect: Minoru Yamasaki. Engineer: Worthington, Skilling, Helle & Jackson. New York, USA, 2000

Misappropriation

left: Former high school that was used as Security Prison 21 (S-21) by the Khmer Rouge from 1975 to 1979. An estimated 17,000 prisoners were held there with only 12 known survivors. The building is now Tuol Sleng Genocide Museum. Phnom Penh, Cambodia, 2003

right: Gymnasium, 21 years after the Chernobyl disaster. Pripiat, Ukraine, 2007

Wear & tear

left: Brick floor in Saint Basil's Cathedral in Red Square. It consists of nine intimate chapels built from 1555 to 1561. Moscow, Russia, 2007

right: Cast iron floor in Saint Basil's Cathedral. Moscow, Russia, 2007

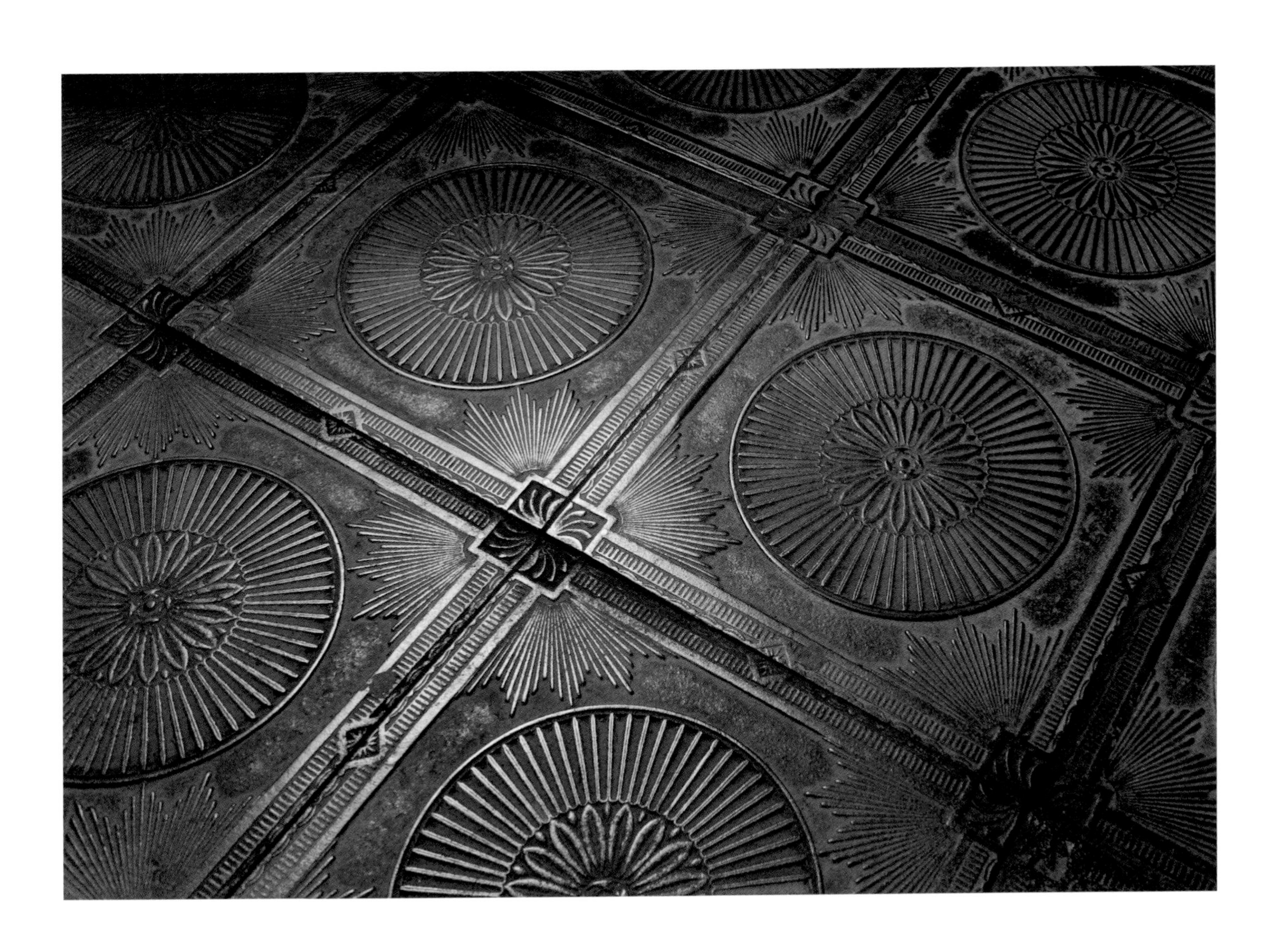

Historic orders

left: Sections of the Berlin Wall, a 140km barrier that completely encircled West Berlin, separating it from East Berlin and the German Democratic Republic (GDR). The wall came to symbolise the Iron Curtain between Western Europe and the Eastern Bloc. Construction began on 13 August 1961. It was torn down on 9 November 1989 and most pieces have since been sold. Berlin, Germany, 1995

right: Hammer and Sickle crest from the Soviet era that ended in 1991. The slogan reads "USSR: Stronghold of Peace". Sculpture Park, Moscow, Russia, 2007

СССРОПЛО

Palimpsest

left: Lightswitch in a bedroom of the Hotel Polissia 21 years after the Chernobyl disaster. Pripiat, Ukraine, 2007

right: Billboard with posters removed at Green Park Underground Station. London, UK, 2009

PARK
GAM
GREEN

Vanishing fresco

left: Concert hall with water-damaged Soviet relief sculpture and piano.
Pripiat, Ukraine, 2007

right: This rapidly decaying rock painting, which may be up to 2000 years old, depicts two elands (antelopes) and two half-animal, half-human shaman figures. Recorded during the Lesotho Rock Art Survey, 2000. Lesobeng Valley, Lesotho, 2000

Architecture as Stage Set

Architecture [is] a theatre stage setting where the leading actors are the people, and to dramatically direct the dialogue between these people and space is the technique of designing.

Kisho Kurokawa

Public places and buildings have the added dimension of acting as arenas for our lives. In the virtual era we have a heightened awareness of the nature of illusion, of the fact that we are at one and the same time both observing and participating. We see buildings as the backdrop to history and human drama, no longer as organic wholes to which we are connected. In a global village we become tourists and visitors to the sets of a world of other cultures. The photographer, always the contriver and exposer of visual illusion, is attuned to this particularly contemporary phenomenon. Cities and places continually present new ironies, making the observer constantly aware of the layers of transparency. People become orchestrated crowds, and architecture a grand theatrical set, yet individuals are still glimpsed, asserting the defiantly human amongst the towering forests of forms.

Between sets

left: Concrete table tennis table outside the Unité d'habitation built in 1963 by Le Corbusier. Briey-en-forêt, France, 2005

right: Concrete table tennis table outside a badgir, the Iranian term for wind tower. These chimney-like structures, which project above the roof, expel warm air during the day and trap cooler breezes at night. Yazd, Iran, 2008

Up to the neck

left: Fibreglass shark sculpture erected in 1986, on the 41st anniversary of the dropping of the first atomic bomb. Created by sculptor John Buckley for Bill Heine, who lives in the house. Neighbours tried to force Heine to remove the shark, but after an appeal to the UK's Secretary of State for the Environment, it was allowed to remain. Oxford, England, 2009

right: Sculpted heads surrounding a front door in Lambeth. London, England, 2009

Architectural snapshot

left: Posing for a photograph in front of the ruins of the gatehouse. Persepolis, Iran, 2008

right: Posing for a photograph by the Dogana di Mare, located at the tip of Dorsoduro. Saint Mark's Basilica and Campanile are visible behind. Venice, Italy, 1991

Nudging neighbours

left: Front doors, Walthamstow. London, UK, 2009

right: Front doors, Walthamstow. London, UK, 2009

385

Scene painting

left: Mural commemorating martyrs of the Iran-Iraq war (1980-1988). It reads "Martyrdom is the art of the men of God". Imam Khomeini" and "Generals Shiroodi and Keshvari". Tehran, Iran, 2008

right: Graffiti in the South Bank Skatepark below the Queen Elizabeth Hall. It is an area of unused architecture that has been used by the skateboarding community since the early 1970s. London, UK, 2009

Space to play

left: Guadalquivir river-front in the evening. Seville, Spain, 1993

right:Rodadero, a huge glacially striated diorite rock opposite Saqsayhuaman, the Inca complex, during Inti Raymi (the festival of the sun). Cuzco, Peru, 2008

Architectural orders

left: Façade of the Stalinist-style Great Hall of the People, which functions as the People's Republic of China's parliament building. It was one of the Ten Great Constructions completed for the tenth anniversary of the People's Republic in September 1959 . It was built in ten months by volunteers. Architect: Zhang Bo. Tiananmen Square, Beijing, China, 2007

right: The Finnish Parliament Building (Eduskuntatalo) built in 1931. Architect: Johan Sigfrid Sirén. Helsinki, Finland, 2007

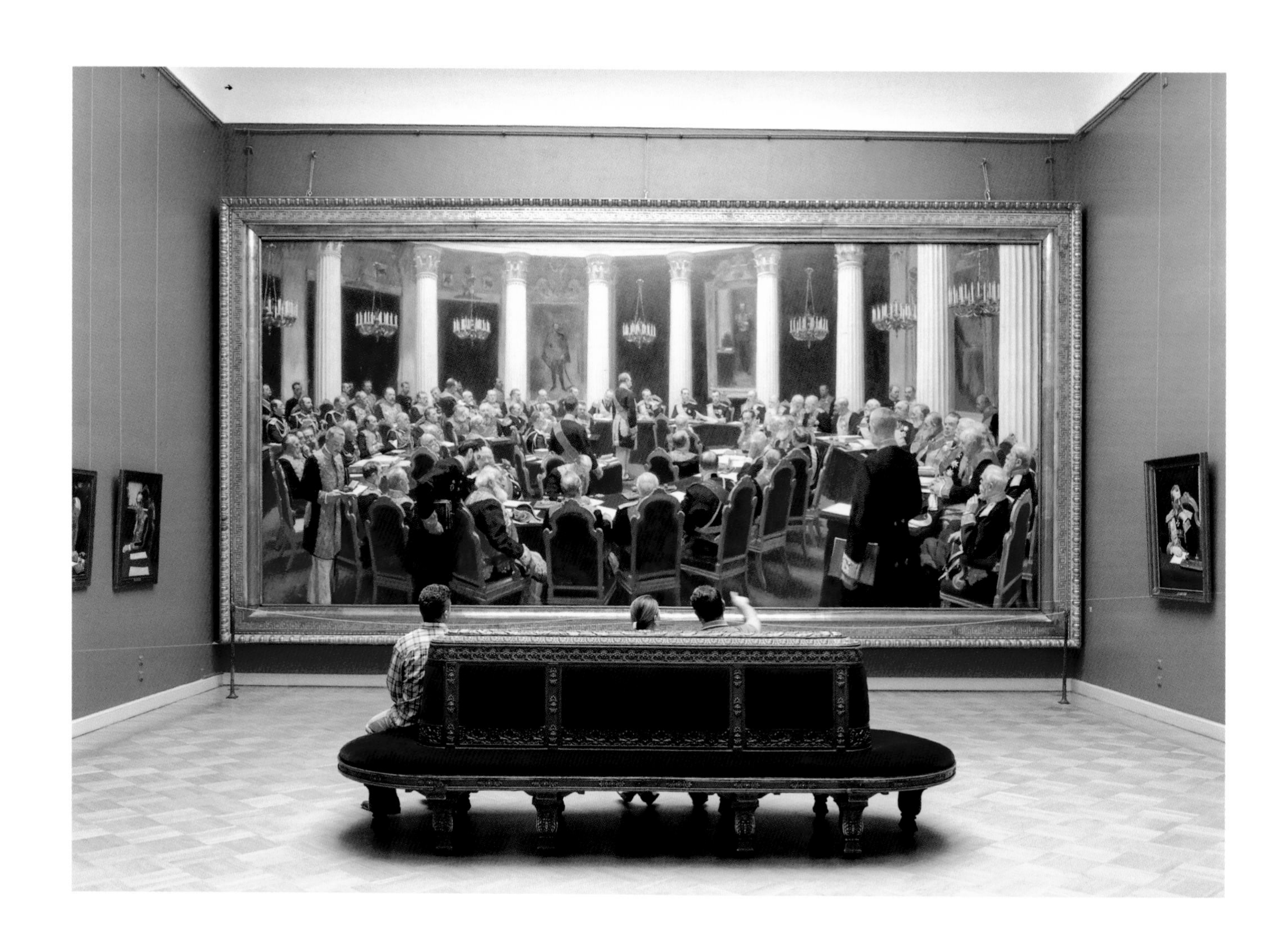

Spectating space

left: Seated viewers in front of *Formal Session of the State Council on May 7, 1901, in honour of the 100th Anniversary of Its Founding* by Ilya Yefimovich Repin, 1903, oil on canvas, State Russian Museum. St. Petersburg, Russia, 2007

right: A tour group outside Injeongjeon Hall (the throne hall), Changdeokgung palace. Originally built 1405, destroyed in the Imjin Wars, restored 1609, destroyed by fire 1803. The current structure dates from 1804. Seoul, Korea, 2007

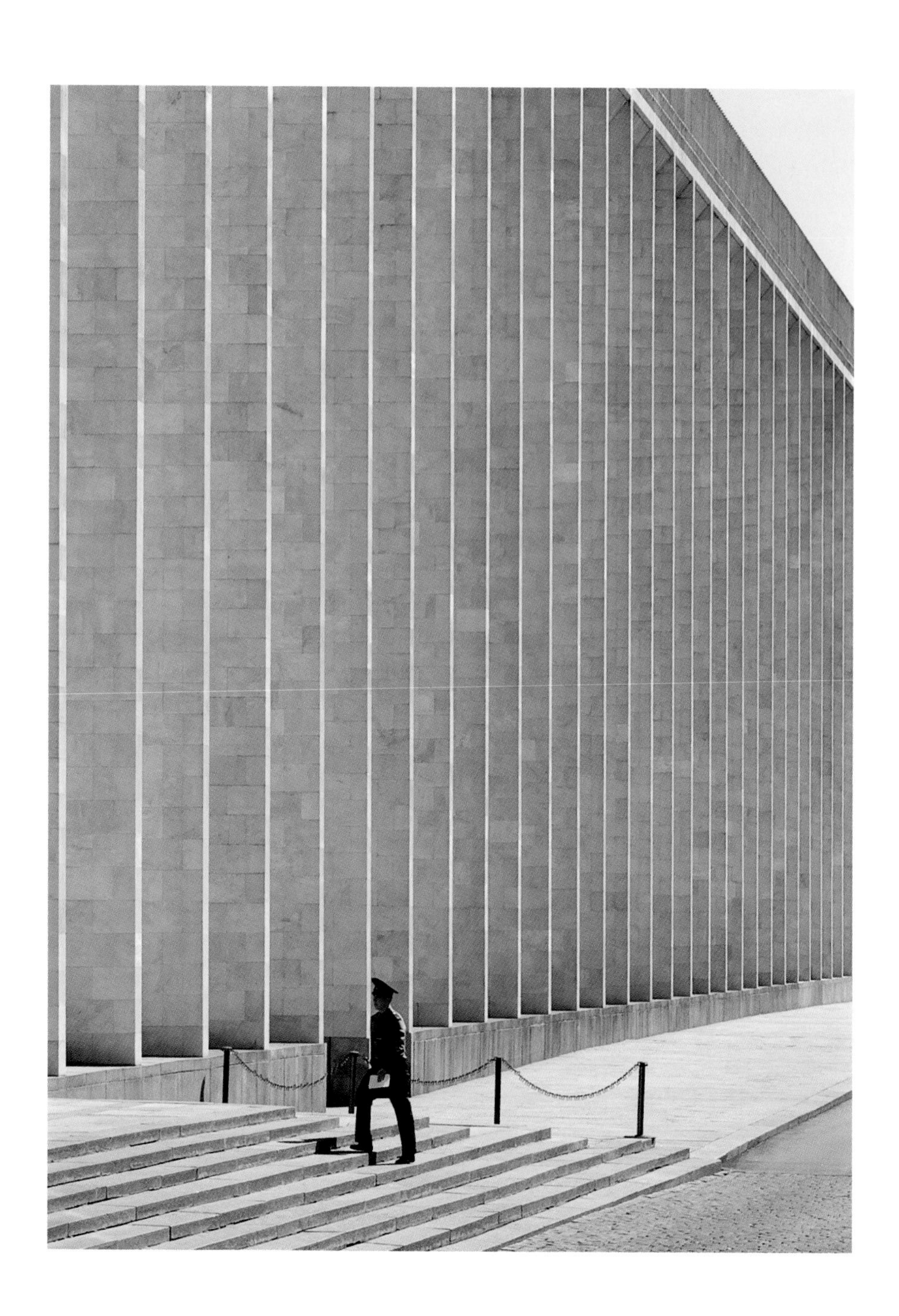

Walking the line

left: An official on the steps of the State Kremlin Palace below the white marble columns. Built 1959-61. Architect: Michael M. Poshokin. Moscow, Russia, 2007

right: Tailani Souza during the filming of *Holidays in Cubatão*, directed by Rubens Azevedo. Cubatão, Brazil, 2008

Urban Horizons

When you look at a city, it's like reading the hopes, aspirations and pride of everyone who built it.

Hugh Newell Jacobsen

The greatest architectural gestures of our civilisation, the very epitome and physical embodiment of that civilisation, the apparently random and chaotic surge of something intended and planned, the phenomenal paradox of achievement and disaster, the home of ultimate construction and destruction, the Twenty-First century city, is outpacing any attempt to define its nature the very second an image is formed of it. How to represent, how to see, how to know, this most mercurial of forms, that constantly defies notions of what is attainable? As a photographer, the emerging conurbations, the fresh unimagined megalopolises demand a perspective. This is a quest for scope. These horizons, where the patterns and grids of vast populations are assembled out of seeming chaos, are a bright optimistic contribution, a means of attempting to see a future that is happening right now.

Constant sky

left: Downtown São Paulo seen from the top of the Edificio Italiano. With a population of eleven million residents São Paulo is the most populous city in the Southern hemisphere. São Paulo, Brazil, 2008

right: Cuzco seen from Christo Blanco. The city has a population of 350,000 and is located at an altitude of 3,300m. Peru, 2008

Haze & Twilight

left: Huangpu River seen from Jin Mao Tower observation deck. Shanghai is the largest city in China in terms of population and one of the largest metropolitan areas in the world, with over 20 million inhabitants. Shanghai, China, 2007

right: Kalyan minaret and Kalyan Mosque Dome. Bukhara is the capital of Bukhara Province of Uzbekistan. It is the nation's fifth largest city, with a population of 238,000. Bukhara, Uzbekistan, 1999

Emerging metropolis

left: Tehran seen from Bam-e-Tehran (the roof of Tehran). Tehran is the largest city in the Middle East and the most populated city in south-west Asia with a population of 7.5 million (approximately 15 million in Greater Tehran). Tehran, Iran, 2008

right: City of London skyline from Sydenham Hill. The city has a population of 7.5 million within the boundaries of Greater London making it the most populous municipality in the European Union. London, UK, 2009

Warp & weft

left: Terracotta rooftops in Bologna seen from the top of the medieval tower Asinelli. The city is the capital of Emilia-Romagna region and has a population of 370,000. Bologna, Italy, 2000

right: Granada, the capital of the province of Granada, has a population of 230,000. It is seen here from the Alhambra. Granada, Spain, 1993

Mountain backdrop

left: With a population of over 10 million Seoul is home to a quarter of South Korea's population and is bordered by eight mountains. Seoul, South Korea, 2007

right: The upmarket Elahieh district of Tehran next to the Alborz mountains. Tehran, Iran, 2008

Implied regulation

left: Midtown Manhattan seen from the Empire State building. New York is the most populous city in the USA with 8.3 million inhabitants, 1.6 million of whom live on Manhattan Island. New York, USA, 1990

right: Dubrovnik, located on the Adriatic Coast, has a population of 44,000. Dubrovnik, Croatia, 2005

Geometric cluster

left: An area of Yongsan-gu, south-west of Namsan Park seen from the Seoul Tower. Seoul, South Korea, 2007

right: Aerial view of the centre of Oxford, which has a population of 165,000. Many of the buildings are part of Oxford University, the oldest university in the English-speaking world. They are recognisable by the golden Cotswold limestone and private Quads (an abbreviation of quadrangle), used to describe a college court completely surrounded by buildings and approached through a gateway. Oxford, UK, 2004

Urban Hinterland

left: Rock-cut dwellings in Cappadocia. Turkey, 1994

right: Chicago looking south from Sears Tower in winter. Chicago, USA, 1999

Paths of least resistance

left: Apartments on Hong Kong Island, which has a population of 1.3 million. Hong Kong, China, 2004

right: A favela developed horizontally into the jungle along the route of the old road used for constructing the highway Cubatão, Brazil, 2008

Ancient dynasties

left: Persepolis was the ceremonial capital of the Persian Empire (550–330 BC) during the Achaemenid dynasty. Persepolis, Iran, 2008

right: Phnom Bakheng was built more than two centuries before Angkor Wat at the end of the 9th century. It was the principal temple of the Angkor region, and a symbolic representation of Mount Meru, home of the Hindu gods.
Siem Reap, Cambodia, 2003

Slicing cities

left: Highway in downtown São Paulo. Brazil, 2008

right: A man ascending an arch of Lupu Bridge over the Huangpu River. Shanghai, China, 2007

Index

Biography

Quintin Lake is a photographer and architect. He studied at the Architectural Association and is a fellow of the Royal Geographical Society and the Royal Society of Arts. He has travelled to over 60 countries with expeditions including Greenland, Lesotho and Peru. Recent solo exhibitions include *Cities and Landscapes*, *Orquideas Interoceanicas* and *Pripiat: 21 Years After Chernobyl*.

www.quintinlake.com

Acknowledgments

Many thanks to my publisher, Alexandra Papadakis, with whom the development of the book has been a true collaboration, not to mention an enjoyable journey. The project would have been impossible without her skills in layout and picture editing and she is directly responsible for many of the headlines and comparisons. My gratitude to the countless builders, architects and engineers whose work has provided the inspiration for this project. My heartfelt thanks also to those whose work has encouraged me to look beyond the surface of things: the teachings of Mark Prizeman and Pascal Schöning; the exhibition *Thinking Aloud* curated by Richard Wentworth; the films *Sans Soleil* directed by Chris Marker, London and *Robinson in Space* directed by Patrick Keiller; the works of photographers Robert Polidori and Stephen Shore; and the books *Architecture without Architects* by Bernard Rudofsky and *For Inspiration Only* by Future Systems. Many thanks to those I have had the pleasure to travel with and those who have supported taught and inspired me in other ways: The AABCC, Alain de Botton, Alan and Alison Berman, Alpha, The Architectural Association, Benedict O'Looney, Beruska, Beverley Wilcox, Bill Dunster, Brian Souter, BSES Expeditions, The Cambridge University Expedition Society, Charterhouse, Chris Dukes, Christopher Reeves, The people of Cubatão, The Dragon School, David Richardson, Earl de Grey, Edward Stancliffe, Fly Agaric and the Woodpeckers, Granville Heptonstall, Hugh Cumming, Hugh Pryor, Julia Massey-Stewart, Pluto, Mark and Suzanna Prizeman, Miki Ando, Mila Fürstová, Mustafa Salman, Naomi Prasad, Nick Mills, Nogol Zahabi, The Oxford University Expedition's Council, Patrick Dupont-Liot, Paul Dobraszczyk, Raleigh International, The RGJ, Richard Crowsley, Richard Scrase, Richard Wentworth, Rob Jonson, Rojia Forouhar Abadeh, Roman Wittmer, Rosa Maria Roman-Cuesta, The Royal Geographical Society, Rubens Azevedo, Rupert Sagar-Musgrave, Sarah Roberts, Shane & Nigel Winser, Sharron Lee, Sheila de Vallée, Simon Aitken, Smaug Abroad, Stefanie Berchtenbreiter-Overbeck, The Tapirs, Tariq Qureshi, Valerie Bennett and Wilderness Medical Training.

Finally warmest thanks to my parents, Susan and John, for their support and encouragement.

Analogue photographs made with Canon EOS 1000N, 600 & 1 cameras with Fuji Velvia, and Kodak Ektar 100 scanned with Nikon Coolscan 5000ED. Digital photographs made with Canon EOS 10D, 5D & 1ds cameras processed in Adobe Lightroom.

Editioned prints are available of the images in this book from the author's website.